✪ An Observe

Embroidery

✆ An Observer's Guide

Embroidery

Meriel Tilling

Line drawings by Barbara Firth

FREDERICK WARNE

Published by Frederick Warne (Publishers) Ltd, 1983
© Frederick Warne (Publishers) Ltd, 1983

ISBN 0 7232 3159 1

Phototypeset by Tradespools Ltd, Frome, Somerset
Printed in Great Britain at the University Press, Cambridge

Contents

page

Embroidery techniques   7

Transferring the design. Framing up. Appliqué. Bead
embroidery. Canvas work. Crewel or Jacobean embroidery.
Counted thread embroidery. Drawn thread and cutwork
embroidery. Metal thread embroidery. Patchwork. Pulled
linen embroidery. Quilting. Smocking. Shadow work.

Stitches   50

Arrowhead. Back. Basket. Braid. Bullion knot. Buttonhole.
Chain. Chevron. Coral. Couching. Cretan. Feather. Fern.
Fishbone. Fly. French knots. Herringbone. Lazy daisy. Long
and short. Overcast. Pinstitch. Punchstitch. Roman. Running.
Satin. Seeding. Sheaf. Split. Stem. Straight. Thorn. Vandyke.
Wave. Wheatear. Spider's web.

Trimmings and finishes   66

Cords. Fringes. Tassels. Pompoms. Other edgings. Hems.
Mitring.

Stockists   79

Embroidery techniques

Embroidery is becoming an increasingly attractive hobby, offering as it does opportunities for personal expression in design and colour over a wide range of techniques. The 'obsessive' embroideress looks at everything with a new eye, and everything from a common-or-garden spanner to a cloud formation or the most delicate seaweed on the rocks has a significance of shape, texture and colour which can give life a new dimension.

Nearly all amateur embroideresses have difficulty with design. They know that something has a visual appeal for them but they do not know how to transform this into a design in another medium. At this stage it is a definite advantage to join a further education class. Teachers in the various embroidery techniques expect to help and encourage their pupils to do their own designs, and attendance at a class can give inspiration to the home embroideress. Do not allow yourself to be put off by that hopeless feeling we have all experienced when looking at other people's beautiful work. We all have to start somewhere!

It is also of great value to the amateur to form her own folio, or scrapbook of ideas. Photographs from newspapers of some striking object, or showing some new angle of approach to an object; colour plates of colour schemes which particularly appeal—anything which may eventually be digested and used as a source of inspiration. Nothing need be used at once; ideas take a long time to mature and come very gradually to the surface of the mind, and I have kept a picture as long as ten years before 'suddenly' having the illumination as to how to treat it!

Another source of help to the striving embroideress is to get into company with others having the same interest. This may seem a truism, but to the beginner to join a specialist society or association can seem presumptuous, and she may hesitate in the same way a tennis 'rabbit' does to join a tennis club. Do not hesitate; join and attend meetings and exhibitions. Keen embroideresses are always prepared to talk about embroidery, about sources of materials, about books and

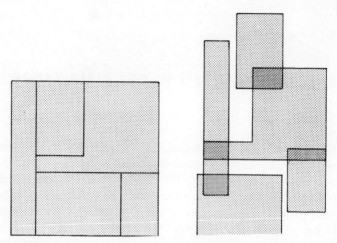

classes, and to share their know-how with anyone else interested. Tips and ideas in quite different techniques may be picked up and stored away mentally for future use as one's interest in the subject widens and becomes more comprehensive.

After that try, and keep trying, to design for yourself. Try cutting paper shapes; try 'exploding' simple geometric shapes; try enlarging 'doodles'; try drawing a very simple outline picture, cutting out the component shapes in coloured tissue paper and arranging and re-arranging them on a background; try simple geometric or natural shapes in different textures or colours; try one simple successful design in different techniques; try using a simple motif from wallpaper or curtain material. Remember that the simpler the design the more scope there probably is for elaborating it with stitchery, texture and colour, without it becoming overdone. Cut out a brown paper 'frame' to lay over the design to judge the relationship of the worked areas to their background.

When you have achieved what you think may be a satisfactory design, prop it up where you will see it as you go about your home, and 'brood' over it. This applies to the work at all stages, particularly when you seem to be stuck for how next to develop your theme. Enlightenment may come from a sudden glimpse of the work when the mind is apparently quite empty of thought on the subject.

Transferring the design

Once the chosen design has been drawn out it can be transferred onto the background material by one of several methods. The traditional method for fine materials is the 'prick and pounce' method. A careful tracing of the design is made, perhaps on greaseproof paper **a**, and turned over onto a folded ironing blanket or clean padding, and the lines of the design are then pricked through the paper with a strong needle **b**, following all the details closely but not allowing the holes to become so close as to tear the paper. When this is completed the drawing is laid right side up on the background material which has been drawing-pinned out, smooth and square, on a board. The design is then pinned onto the background in position and pounced through.

Pounce may be light or dark as appropriate for dark or light fabrics, and consists of powdered chalk or powdered charcoal, obtainable from a chemist. Using a small roll, or pad, of felt, spread a little of the appropriate pounce along the lines of the design, pressing it gently through the holes **c**. When the whole design has been pounced, remove the tracing and a very fine outline of powder spots can be seen. Naturally the size of the needle used as a pricker will have determined the size of these outline spots. Taking care not to rub them off, paint along the lines with a fine brush in water colour **d**. When the paint is dry puff off any remaining powder.

An alternative to this method is to lay a tracing of the design over

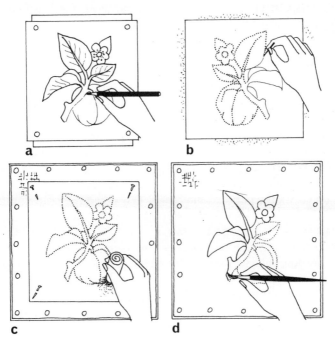

the background, and tack around the outlines through both layers. Then tear off the paper leaving the tacking outlines on the background. This can be successful with fairly simple outline shapes, but the worker may have problems with fine details. On the other hand the design so transferred may be slightly altered or adapted in the working, which may not be possible with the prick and pounce method as the paint is not easy to get off a delicate fabric and will have to be covered with stitchery.

Transparent materials such as organdie can be used as tracing paper themselves, laid over the design, and the drawing transferred onto the material with a hard sharp pencil (3H).

Canvas work designs can be drawn out lightly onto squared paper of the same number of squares to the inch as the canvas has holes or threads to the inch, and then the outlines can be squared off. This then gives the worker a precise master pattern to follow, each square representing one stitch. Or the design can be drawn through the canvas using the canvas as tracing paper, and then be painted over with waterproof ink—waterproof so that, if the finished work has to be damped and stretched, the design lines do not run onto the wools. This is not very easy when the canvas is a fine close weave but can be made easier by placing the tracing and canvas against a window. The light then shows up the design more clearly.

Framing up

When the work has to be done in a frame, the frame used should be appropriate for the work. For instance shadow work, or drawn threadwork can be done in a ring frame, but metal thread embroidery or canvas work need to be more permanently framed in a rectangular frame which can be bought or made at home. Some kinds of embroidery require a firm cotton backing to the background material, and this should be attached before framing up. It must be carefully tacked on by the grain of the fabric, first down the centre, and then across the centre, and then dissected as many more times as seems desirable for the size of the work **a**.

If the work is going to be mounted in the frame with drawing pins, it may be desirable to protect the edges of fine materials or loosely woven materials. For this purpose the edges may be bound with some clean cotton fabric to protect them against the pull of the drawing-pins **b**, or strips of felt may be laid on the wooden frame under the background before pinning it on. Great care must be taken to get the

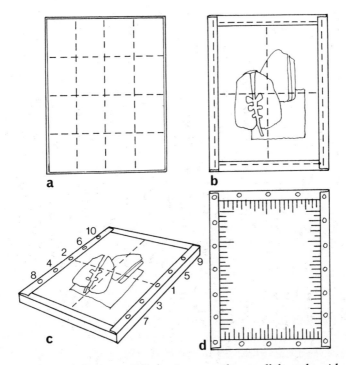

a   b

c   d

straight grain of the material running exactly parallel to the sides of the frame. Then the material may be pinned on **c**. Start at the middle of one side, and put in one pin. Then pinning tightly, put in a pin in the middle of the opposite side. Work outwards to the corners, first a pin one side then a pin the other side, pulling tightly and keeping the work even all the time. One cannot over-emphasize the need for the material to be accurately and tautly mounted ready for working. When doing metal thread embroidery an extra row of tacking stitches is advisable at this stage. Now that the work is tautly mounted, work a row of long stitches at right angles to the sides of the frame, and of uneven length **d**. Again work them outwards from the middle of each side to the corners. These will be a final insurance that the pull on the two background materials will be even.

If, when completed, a piece of work is to be mounted as a panel it must then be stretched firmly over a hardboard backing. If the piece of work is on fine material, or as with metal thread embroidery has certain unevennesses on the back where the thick threads have come through, pad the hardboard with thin old blanket or flannel first. This may be stuck onto the hardboard over the edges and prevents the

5

finished work looking too flat and mean. Over this lay the work. Then, with a needle threaded with a very long length of button thread, lace the work together across the back both ways, beginning at the centres and making sure to keep the work square with the mount. Take particular care at the corners to turn them over neatly and not create a bulky lump. Successive lengths of thread may be tied onto the last. Keep the work pulled nice and tight, but take care not to pull so tightly as to tear the thread through the fabric.

*   *   *

Although the different embroidery techniques below are discussed separately, one of the great joys of modern needlework is that different techniques can be, and are, used together today in a way which would hardly have been possible in days gone by. Thus a technique such as appliqué can be used in conjunction with needle-weaving and gold-work, and all three are enriched thereby. Because of this, even if the embroideress wants to specialize in some technique which particularly appeals to her, it is as well to have tried out more than one in order to be able to combine them to greater effect. This is not to say that restraint and simplicity are not also very desirable, and embroidery in one colour and one technique must always have a particular charm. It is perhaps a trait of modern embroidery that we incline to overdo our effects, piling on more and more stitchery, and prizing richness too highly. It is a great advantage to be able to know where to stop!

Some of the methods of embroidery described are not often used today. This is a pity. Embroidery like everything else is subject to the fluctuations of fashion, and crazes for one or other type of embroidery which seem to give us a particularly rewarding outlet from the pressures of modern life seem inevitable. But what beauty and what fascination there is in them all! No doubt it is not wise to be a jack of all trades and master of none, but try them all, master them all and you will find one suitable for every mood. You will not be 'landed' with too many goldwork panels and no table linen, too many quilts and no cushion covers!

Appliqué

Appliqué is a method of embroidery by which shapes cut out in one kind of fabric are applied to a background of another tone, and perhaps a different fabric. The applied shapes form the decoration in themselves, by the contrast in tone with the background, and need not necessarily be enriched by any further stitchery. Depending on the fabrics used, however, the edges of the cut shapes may be covered and strengthened with a cord or stitchery as part of their attachment to the background fabric.

Traditionally appliqué was most often worked on rich fabrics such as velvet, satin or silk, but nowadays it is more commonly worked in linen, or other closely woven fabrics; leather can be used to great effect. It is a particularly suitable form of decoration for achieving a bold effect with simple decorative shapes, and worked in this way it can be very effective on a bedspread or on a hanging. By contrast it is also used on finer articles such as table linen, and also on fine lingerie. Here its particular effectiveness lies in the simple dramatic contrast between the applied motifs or borders and the plain background. There is plenty of scope for the use of appliqué as a decoration on modern dress.

The technique of appliqué requires that the design shall be transferred twice. First the complete design is transferred to the background material where it determines the position of the applied shapes; and then also onto the subsidiary materials out of which the applied shapes are to be cut. To achieve a good flat result without puckering, the background material must be held in a frame while the pieces are attached. Cut out the shapes to be applied with great care so that the grain lies with that of the background. Here there will be a difference depending on the method of attachment. If the edges of the shapes are to be turned in, they must be cut fractionally—0·5 cm ($\frac{1}{4}''$)—larger than the design shapes to allow for this. The shapes are then pinned and tacked onto the relevant part of the background. The worker may either tack them down roughly within the turning line and turn the edge in only as the work proceeds; or tack the turning under close to the edge and then take out the tacking a stitch or two ahead of the hemming. Shapes which have had their edges turned under and invisibly hemmed to the background will probably not require any further embellishment of the edge. This is obviously a suitable method for an article which will be washed fairly frequently, or where the shapes are of a not-too-thick patterned fabric such as might form the appliqué on a bedspread.

Where the appliqué is not going to have the edges turned under, the shapes may be tacked on and then oversewn in place with small stitches. Here it is an advantage to iron them onto an iron-on stiffening first to prevent fraying. This edge can later be covered by a couched thread or cord, or by a line of stitchery such as buttonholing, flat satin stitch, or chain stitch. The cord, or stitching, covers the cut edge of the shape and both protects it from fraying and further decorates it.

Appliqué on lingerie may have the edges turned in finely and pinstitched or punchstitched (see page 59). In this case the shapes may be tacked onto the background and the tacking removed a stitch or two in advance of the pinstitching. Alternatively, the second layer for the applied shapes may be laid in its entirety over the background, and have the design transferred on to it. The outline of the design is then punchstitched (see page 60) through both layers, and afterwards the surplus material is cut away very close to the edge of the stitching. This method is also appropriate for applying lace onto a garment or handkerchief. This same method of applying the whole piece with the design on it onto the background and embroidering over the outlines, this time in buttonhole or flat satin stitch, and then cutting away the surplus of the top layer, is also used when applying onto net. The applied piece may alternatively be applied *underneath* the background and then after stitching the background is cut away from on top.

In all cases where there is a very obvious grain in the applied fabric it should lie with the grain of the background material as this helps to prevent puckering. This rule can of course be broken in order to create some special effect, but this should only be done knowingly and with intent.

Another variation of appliqué is called inlay. In this case the shapes are cut out of the background and another fabric is inlaid in to the cut out hole. Extreme care must be taken to match hole and applied shape, and it is best if possible to cut both together with a Stanley knife. The edges of the new piece and of the hole are then oversewn together. This is probably best done with the background fabric and the filling pieces tacked in position onto a backing such as brown paper. If leather is being used, the pieces should not be tacked but very lightly stuck, with a central dab of glue, onto the backing. Take care to use a non-marking glue such as Pritt. Care must be taken not to sew into this backing, which of course is removed after the stitching is completed. The edge may have a couched thread or a cord sewn on over it as a finishing decoration.

(For stitches see section on Stitches, page 50)

Bead embroidery

Bead embroidery is, perhaps more than most kinds of embroidery, subject to changing taste and styles in fashion. Some of its fascination lies in the intrinsic charm of the beads themselves. Bead embroidery on canvas enjoyed a great vogue in the Victorian era, and has considerable period charm. Beads were sewn onto canvas, each bead taking the place of one tent, or half cross stitch. In this way geometric designs or pictorial subjects were enriched and saved from monotony by the incorporation into parts of the design of beads of differing colours, but all of one size. Many of these attractive embroideries survive, although they may be in need of repair.

Another kind of bead embroidery which enjoys a periodic popularity is bead weaving. This technique is inherited from the North American Indians, and the weaving is done on a bead loom which can be bought, or can be made at home out of a strong cardboard box or polystyrene tray. The diagram shows such a box with notches made at each end. Again beads of one size must be used, and preferably beads with smooth rounded edges. A flat piece of beading is then produced into which a design worked out on squared paper can be introduced. Belts, necklets and bracelets can be made in this way, and with ingenuity the same technique can be used for covering boxes and making bags.

On a home-made bead loom the warp thread is tied round the first upright and the end can be made secure with Sellotape. Then wind the thread round the uprights at either end alternately so as to form 'V's and fasten it onto the final upright **a**. Then tie one thread around these warp threads bringing them closer together and more nearly parallel.

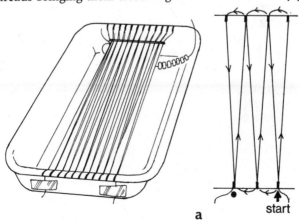

a

start

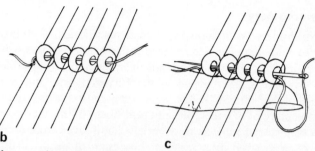

b   **c**

Thread a very long thread into a beading needle and tie the end onto the first warp thread. Thread as many beads as there are spaces between the warp threads onto the needle. Running *under* the warp threads, bring the threaded beads up against the warp threads so that one bead comes in between each warp thread **b**. Then take the needle *over* the top of the warp threads and, coming back, pick up each bead again and thread it onto the needle thus holding them each in their respective place in the weft **c**. When the thread runs out thread it back through part of the previous row of beads. Do the same with the new thread. A pattern worked out in colour on squared paper may be transferred to the weaving, each coloured square representing one coloured bead. Do remember, however, when working out your design that the beads are *not* square, but that they are taller than they are wide as they lie in the finished work, and allowances must be made for this in a design.

A third form of bead embroidery is the use of the beads for their own sake, instead of stitchery, in an arrangement of colour and texture. A simple outline shape or pattern may be padded with cord and then covered, and piled up with beads of many hues and tones in what is in fact an 'orderly disorder'. This kind of embroidery requires a store or reservoir of beads of many sizes, shapes and varieties. Old beads can be picked up at jumble sales and markets; new beads are found at certain specialist shops. A combination of the two is best, as modern beads incline to be glittery and hard-looking, although they can be bought with clear glass, opaque, china or wooden surfaces. Motifs or simple patterns made rich when worked in beads can be used on evening wear, bags, belts and boxes.

The most common use for beads is in combination with other embroidery techniques. Beads are nearly always used in conjunction with metal thread embroidery, and are quite often incorporated into modern canvas work. They are not a regular part of the pattern, as in Victorian times, but highlight certain parts of the design, or give a different texture to the work. They also combine well with appliqué on leather or rich fabrics.

When using beads in embroidery the thread with which they are sewn must always be strengthened by rubbing with beeswax. The thread itself may be linen button thread for canvas work, or pure silk, but it must be strengthened as this helps to prevent any cutting edge in the beads prematurely wearing the thread. A ball of beeswax should be kept in the work-box, and the length of silk pulled against it down its whole length several times before being threaded into the needle. The kind of needle used will depend on the type of embroidery and the type of beads. For sewing beads onto canvas a strong button thread in a tapestry needle will be satisfactory with wooden beads, but many glass beads have very fine holes, and beading needles which are obtainable in mixed sizes are essential. These needles are very long and have very fine eyes, which in the finer sizes will pass through the finest beads. Being very long, several beads can be picked up and threaded at once, which is useful when bead weaving and when working beads over string padding.

A good idea when working with beads is to line a lid with velvet or felt to use as a container for the few working beads. This stops them skidding and jumping about, and getting lost.

Canvas work

Working on canvas must have been one of the most permanently popular forms of embroidery throughout the centuries, and most of our museums and country houses contain examples of the work of our ancestors. In past time canvas work was used for the embellishment of furniture and furnishings, chair seats, foot stools, kneelers and cushions, but today hangings and wall panels enjoy considerable popularity, as well as lamp bases, bags, and articles of dress. Whatever the article the warm tones of wool, which is the usual medium, and the enduring strength of the material make it a most rewarding form of embroidery.

There is a considerable range of canvas available from the coarsest of double thread canvas suitable for rugs, to the finest single thread canvas suitable for evening bags worked in silk. Canvas is numbered so many holes to the inch. The coarseness of the canvas will determine the type of wool and the number of strands of wool to be used in the needle as the required effect is obtained by completely covering the background with the worked wool stitches. On the whole a single thread canvas is preferable to a double as all stitches may be worked on this, but not all stitches may be worked on double canvas. Care should be taken with the wool used. It is always a pity to expend a great deal of time and work with poor materials, and a good quality will be worth the extra money in softness and depth of colour, and in durability. There are several ranges available from stockists listed at the back of the book. Canvas work is done with tapestry needles. These are available in several sizes; they are blunt needles with large eyes suitable for working on a 'pre-holed' material using a comparatively thick thread.

The universally recognized 'tapestry' work—(which is in fact a misnomer from weaving)— is that done in tent stitch, half stitch or cross stitch, the same stitch being used throughout, and the only variation lying in the shading of the colours. Tent stitch worked on single thread canvas is known as *petit point*, and cross stitch on double canvas as *gros point*. For this work canvas can be bought with a design ready painted on it. More costly are designs which are sold ready 'trammed'. This means that the design has horizontal threads in the appropriate places so that the embroideress can easily follow the design and need not use so many strands of wool in her needle for working the tent stitch. The background is then probably worked in a thicker cheaper kind of wool.

The first step forward for the amateur embroideress is to work from a squared paper chart. This allows her to translate the design into colours of her own choice or, of course, to follow the colour key provided. From there she may progress to drawing her own design; first, perhaps a simple geometric design drawn straight on to the squared paper, later, a freer design, squared up as a second stage. Of course it takes longer to get started if you produce your own 'home-made' design, but the satisfaction in the work will be infinitely greater.

Nowadays embroideresses have come to realize that there are many more stitches available and suitable for use in canvas embroidery, and that their design can be greatly enhanced by the use of a variety of stitches. Again we must be careful not to proliferate stitches just for the sake of showing that we have them in our armoury, but a certain variety can add depth and texture to an otherwise flat surface.

When designing for an article of furniture particular care must be taken to make the design fit the area to be filled. Home-made designs often come 'unstuck' because they are designed without attention to their relation to the article. If a rhomboid chair seat is to be worked, it is better to draw a rhomboid design for it. This then looks as though it has been worked for that particular chair, whereas a small circular pattern will not look so effective. This is in fact a general truth about designing, but it seems to need particular emphasis when considering designs for furniture.

Another point to be remembered is that canvas is very liable to distortion, particularly if a large area of tent stitch is to be worked. The work must therefore be mounted in a frame, and kept stretched quite taut throughout the working process. If a piece of work is too large for your frame, a commercial frame will allow for the surplus canvas to be rolled over the horizontal end bar while the first part is worked; then that part can be rolled away and the surplus rolled into the working position.

When completed the work will require stretching to achieve a good smooth finish. This is done by placing several layers of wet blotting paper on a wooden board and laying the work face downwards on it. With the straight edges parallel with the grain, pin first one side and then the other, as was done when mounting the work in the frame. When the work has been well stretched and pinned on all round, it can be left to dry for twenty-four hours or so, at room temperature, before taking out the pins. If for any reason the work has become badly distorted, this stretching process may have to be repeated several times to correct it.

Although wool has been mentioned particularly in connection with canvas work, other threads have been combined with wool in the past, and very frequently are today. Small areas of stranded cotton or silk will give a highlight to the soft tones of wool which is very pleasing. In the same way the textures of beads, string and raffia may contribute to the interest of the design.

Some useful canvas stitches are shown below.

Tent stitch   This stitch is very easily mistaken for half cross stitch but is worked differently and makes a much thicker and more compact cover of the canvas. It is worked from right to left or can be worked

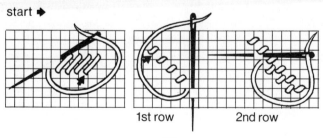

start ➡

1st row   2nd row

diagonally. It is usually worked diagonally when large areas are to be covered as this is less inclined to distort the canvas. The back has long stitches. At the end of a row the work can be turned upside down for the return journey.

Half cross stitch   As will be seen from the diagram this has only a short vertical stitch behind the canvas. It can be worked in either direction.

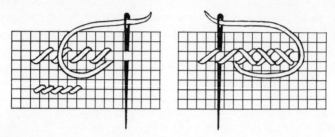

Cross stitch   This completes half cross stitch by making the return journey across the first. This doubles the vertical stitches on the back. All the stitches in the first row must lie in the same direction, and all the stitches on top must also lie in the same direction.

Long armed cross stitch

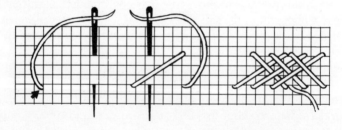

Fishbone stitch   The second row is worked upside down.

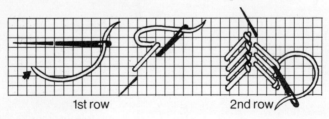

1st row   2nd row

Gobelin stitch and Upright gobelin stitch

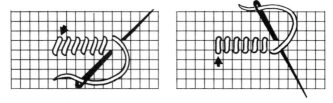

Plaited gobelin stitch

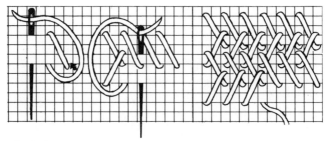

Knotted stitch

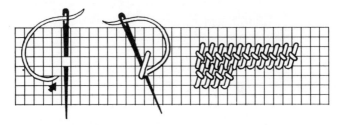

Rice stitch This stitch can be worked very effectively in two colours. The arms of the large cross stitch being crossed with another colour (below, left).

Algerian eye stitch (right)

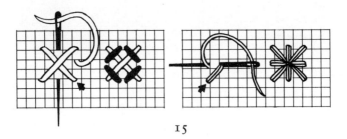

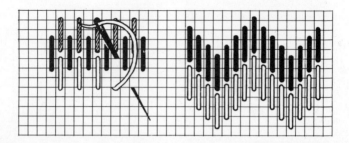

Florentine stitch This stitch can be worked all over in a variety of patterns. The basic stitch is shown in the diagram above, followed by a simple arrangement. The sketches below show different arrangements of stitch. Each successive row is worked exactly the same in a different shade of one colour; up to four or five shades may be used. The gently graduated shades contribute a subtly tonal effect. The last sketch shown can be shaded within the rectangles or each rectangle or row of rectangles shaded differently.

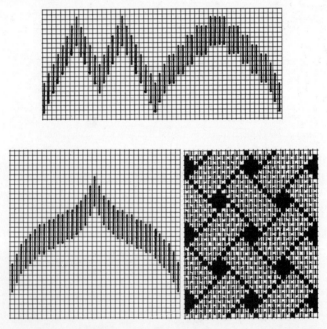

A specialized form of canvas work is rug-making. Needle-made rugs can be made in a variety of stitches to give flat or pile effects. Cross stitch and Soumak stitch **a** are flat stitches, and Surrey stitch **b** is a pile

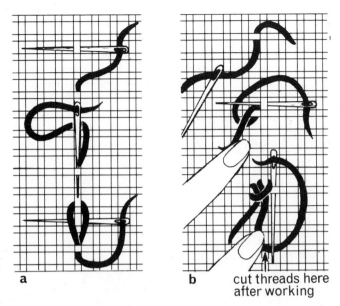

<table>
<tr><td>a</td><td>b</td><td>cut threads here
after working</td></tr>
</table>

stitch. Designs can be worked out on squared paper in the same way as for other canvas work, and the scale and fineness of the work can be chosen to suit the taste of the worker. A short pile rug in the glowing colours of superior quality wool is an heirloom indeed!

Crewel or Jacobean embroidery

Crewel embroidery is a traditional kind of embroidery using surface stitches in wool on a linen background, and usually with floral designs, sometimes incorporating animals. The style of the floral designs has varied in different centuries, and examples of bed hangings, curtains, cushions and table covers may be found in many of our great houses and in museums. Crewel, in fact, refers to the particular kind of wool thread used and should therefore be used to describe wool embroidery. Jacobean refers to the style of design particularly popular in the seventeenth century. The same kind of embroidery however was worked in a rather later period in silk or cotton threads. Perhaps the greatest periods of this kind of embroidery were during the sixteenth to the eighteenth centuries.

The background material for wool embroidery of this type is usually a linen twill, but any strong pre-shrunk material may be used. When using silks in place of wools linen may be used for the background, or a furnishing satin of good strong quality. The background is usually neutral in colour as this gives an ideal contrast to the embroidery in which colour in soft shades and tones is one of the predominant features. The traditional crewel wools—fine 2 ply worsted wool—are available in a marvellous range of beautiful colours in soft gradations of shades; stranded silks are only available imported from abroad and are expensive, but stranded cottons can be used. The more intense colour of the cottons gives a different result from wools but can be quite satisfactory in its own way. Crewel needles are of course particularly suitable for this kind of work; they are sharp, pointed needles, but with a long eye, and come in different sizes appropriate to different threads and different numbers of strands. Surface embroidery of this kind should be done in a frame, but a ring frame can be used provided the already worked surface is not spoilt when the frame is tightened.

The traditional leaf and flower shapes are usually filled with different 'filling' stitches such as variations of couching with detached chain and french knots, and are then outlined with chain, whipped chain, stem stitch or split stitch. Sometimes whole leaves or flowers are worked in long and short stitch, carefully shaded. There is a great variety of stitches and their combinations open to the embroideress, although sometimes great effect can be created with only one or two stitches.

So well known is this English tradition of rather quaint floral and animal designs that they have been copied over and over again, and are still available commercially, often used on firescreens and other smaller and less time-consuming articles than the original hangings or other large articles. The technique of surface stitchery in a variety of shades can be used however with quite different and more modern styles of design. Where Jacobean and other period embroidery has flowers joined in flowing curves, modern design tends to prefer a more angular treatment, and prefers a more concentrated area of interest to an 'all-over' design.

Nevertheless, embroidery is for the embroideress and for her setting of it, and to work a beautiful piece of traditional embroidery in a period style may give the embroideress a mastery of colour and stitch which she can go on to use in a less conventional way.

For stitches see section on Stitches, page 50.

Counted thread embroidery

Under this heading I have grouped four techniques worked on linen by the thread. They have been used as a decoration on articles of dress in many national costumes, and for household articles such as cushions, and table linen which need fairly constant washing. Those we shall consider here are cross stitch, assisi embroidery, double running and blackwork. All these styles of counted thread embroidery have earned a lasting popularity over the centuries, and recur in many countries in many different variations.

The requirement common to them all is a basic fabric in which the warp and weft threads are so even in weave that stitches worked either way over the same number of warp or weft threads are indistinguishable in size. The most popular fabric throughout the centuries must have been linen, and counted thread embroidery makes a bold and effective decoration on a monochrome background which is justifiably and enduringly popular. There are also, however, wool weaves, flannel weaves and cotton weaves, and man-made fibres too, which are sufficiently even for counted thread work, and no embroideress need feel impelled to restrict herself to any one type of fabric. Blunt-ended tapestry needles are best used for this work, as they can be inserted between the threads of the fabric, without damaging them and so causing ugly little irregularities. These needles are available in different sizes suitable for different thicknesses of embroidery thread. The work must be held in a frame and a ring frame is quite efficient for this. The needle must be inserted through the material in one movement, and back again through the material in a second movement if the stitches are to achieve the best evenness and a regular tension.

1 **Cross stitch** is perhaps the most popular of all these stitches. As its name implies, the thread first crosses diagonally over one or more warp and weft threads, and then crosses diagonally the other way over the first stitch. Where a large area of cross stitch is to be worked, a whole row of half cross stitches may be worked first and then the whole row be 'crossed' on the return journey. In this way the stitches on the back of the work will all be vertical, and not higgledy-piggledy, which would spoil the finished appearance of the back.

The chief technical requirement of cross stitch, however, is that the stitches on the right side should all be crossed in the same direction, i.e. with the underneath stitch always going from left to right, and the top stitch always going from right to left, or vice versa. If this is not done in even a few instances you get a surprisingly obvious and noticeable ridge effect. The second technical nicety is the tension. This should result in all the stitches being pulled to just the same firmness,

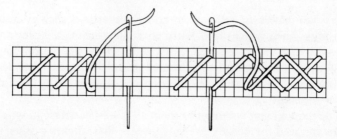

and all the stitches being crossed in exactly the centre of the first stitches. Because the effect of the stitch is so simple, the requirement of even tension is more stringent.

Designs for cross stitch can be worked out on squared paper in exactly the same way as for canvas work. Simple geometric designs in one or two colours can be worked on a neutral background, or in a light colour or white on a striking darker colour. Attractive and more complicated naturalistic designs of birds and flowers using more colours are available, from Scandinavia in particular, and the embroideress can try her hand at a bought design first perhaps, then at a design of her own.

Cross stitch can be combined with other simple stitches as satin stitch, also done by counting the threads that the stitch is worked over, to form many delightful all-over or border designs.

2 **Double running or holbein stitch** consists of a simple running stitch *over* and *under* a regular and repeating number of threads of the background. The pattern line is filled in on the return journey by the running stitch this time going *under* and *over* the same threads to form an unbroken line on the front, and the back, of the work. Traditionally this stitch was worked in black on a white or neutral ground, but there is no particular reason why the embroideress should not use any colour which pleases her or suits her need. This stitch can be, and often is, combined with all or any one, of the other stitches in this section.

3 **Assisi embroidery** is really a combination of cross stitch and double running, but in this case the background of the design is completely worked in cross stitch leaving the design motif in relief, as it were, and this motif is outlined in double running stitch. The double running outline of the motifs is often in a strongly contrasting colour.

Cross stitch decoration is nearly always a partial decoration in that it consists of motifs or a border design, and in this it contrasts with assisi work. The bands of cross stitch, or the areas of colour, show up and are enhanced because of their relation to their background. Therefore it is important when designing for this stitch to pay particular attention to the balance and interrelation of the design and its background. In exactly the *reverse* way an assisi design must show a balance between the light motifs and the strongly coloured cross stitch background.

4 Blackwork was also traditionally worked in black on a white or natural background, and it is often enriched by the addition of touches of couched gold thread. Today sprayed ink can also be used to give the background linen a tone effect before stitching. Blackwork consists of an enormous variety of different filling stitch patterns, very often in double running, or back stitch, and often incorporating cross stitch. Traditionally these filling stitches are worked first and then an outline to the different areas of filling is worked in an outline stitch, such as stem stitch or whipped chain. Nowadays the outlines are not always worked. The chief beauty and skill of this work lies in balancing the tonal differences in the different fillings and many people feel that if the contrasts in weight and scale and tone between different areas are sufficient they do not always require or benefit from the precision of an outline. Designing for blackwork requires fairly clear bold shapes in order to have a sufficient area for each filling used to give it full value in the design. Although traditionally a gold thread is sometimes introduced into the design on Elizabethan blackwork, some other striking colour contrast may be equally effective.

Remember that tonal variety may be multiplied by working different stitches in different thicknesses of black thread—varying from fine man-made poly-cotton thread, through button thread, to coton-à-broder and cotton pearl. The tone can also be varied by using these different threads within the area of one stitch. The result can be striking tonal variation. Blackwork can also be used experimentally and less accurately, even freely, to produce exciting photographic landscapes.

Drawn thread and cutwork embroidery

The distinction between these forms of embroidery is a fine one, and so they have been grouped together. In all of them the effect is achieved by the pattern of light and dark made by the cut or drawn threads. The differences mainly lie in the treatment of the spaces on which depends the emphasis of the design.

This type of embroidery is nearly always worked on linen or cotton, or some firm linen-type fabric where the threads can be cut or withdrawn without prejudicing too much the wearing quality of the garment or article. Obviously if some of the ground is removed this must to some extent weaken the fabric, hence the need for a firm fabric, and for care in design so that the areas so removed or weakened do not out-balance the remainder.

1 **Broderie Anglaise** does not really belong to either of these classes! It consists of a pattern of *pierced* holes, but the basic design lies in the pattern of 'dark' holes against a white background. Areas of padded satin stitch in matching and complementary motifs often link the parts of the design. This form of embroidery was particularly popular in Victorian times when ladies and children wore blouses and dresses pierced all over with patterns of round or oval holes. These holes are first outlined in running stitch then, depending on the size, pierced with a stiletto or cut with fine scissors, and the edge of the hole overcast over the running stitch with satin stitch. Buttonhole is not so commonly used except on the edges or hems of the garments, which were frequently scalloped. The embroidery was worked in white on some firm cotton material, and pierced patterns of great width were worked from the button-holed scalloped hem right up to the waist on children's dresses.

When the hole is small and compact a stiletto can be used; when the hole is larger, say over 4 mm ($\frac{3}{16}''$), or oval, cut the centre in four slashes to the running stitch outline. These flap sections are then folded back underneath and overcast as in the case of the smaller holes, and any surplus on the back cut away close to the overcasting afterwards.

It is unlikely that anyone today would appreciate a garment so worked over as some of these period pieces, but again there is a potential modern use of this technique on for instance blouses or bridesmaids' dresses.

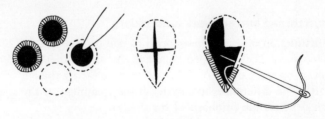

2 Hardanger embroidery is a traditional Norwegian folk embroidery worked on medium weight even linens, often with double threads. It is most useful for table linen and other household articles, although the inventive embroideress can also use it on garments. Groups of threads are withdrawn, alternatively with groups of threads left, to form a trellis pattern within outline borders of rectangular satin stitch blocks. You therefore get a balance of area of cut threads with a plain or decorated trellis design and the contrast of the heavier satin stitch borders.

Double thread Hardanger linen is available at specialist needlework shops, as are designs ready worked out for the embroideress. Once she has had a little experience of the work, however, she may readily work out her own designs.

The rectangular satin stitch blocks are worked first to outline the areas where the threads are to be cut and drawn. A tapestry needle is

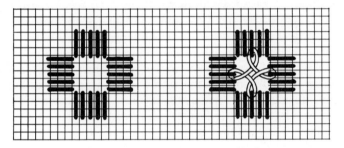

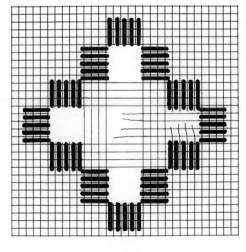

used and the satin stitch is usually worked in a glossy thread of at least the thickness of the material's thread. The satin stitch is worked over four threads in blocks of five stitches, or over six threads in blocks of seven stitches. The blocks are set first horizontally, then vertically. In this way an even number of threads lie between the blocks forming a square in the centre.

If small motifs are worked, all the threads in the square in the centre of the satin stitch will be cut and withdrawn leaving a hole. The withdrawn threads are cut off very carefully on the back as close up to the edge of the satin stitch as possible so that they do not show as an ugly whiskery fringe. This hole may be left as a space or it may be filled with a lacy blanket stitch filling.

Small motifs need to be combined with larger ones for the purpose of forming a design, and larger motifs are built up by the satin stitch blocks being arranged in steps first horizontally, then vertically, to create a larger area for withdrawing the threads. When a larger unit has to be created by the satin stitch outlines, *some* only of these threads within are withdrawn, and some are left. As will be seen in the lower diagram on page 23, the warp and weft threads withdrawn run the same way as the satin stitch block in which they terminate; those left run under the line of the satin stitches. Thus a trellis of threads and spaces is formed. The 'trellis' thread bars can be overcast **a** or needlewoven **b**, in a rather finer firmer thread than that used for the satin stitch. The woven bars are most satisfactorily worked by bringing the needle up in the centre of the group of four threads forming the bar, passing over two on one side and up in the centre,

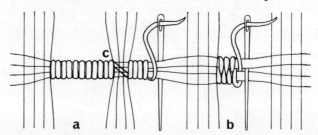

and then passing over the other two and up in the centre again. The needle passes behind the little solid squares where the bars meet and intersect **c**. Further refinements on the trellis bars are little picots worked into the edge of the woven bars on the centre of the bar. These picots are worked as in diagram **d** and are then anchored by passing the thread across in front of the loop thus formed, bringing the needle behind and then up and under the two threads of the bar. Repeat on the other side of the bar.

A knot picot e is worked by bringing the needle point up in the centre of the four threads, twisting the working thread two or three times round the needle and then pulling the thread through these loops. Next take the needle over the top of the two threads of the bar thus pulling the knot picot to the outside, and then bring the needle up in the centre again. The lacy stitch f can be worked on the trellis bars when the last side of the square is half completed. For order of working bars and lacy filling see diagram g.

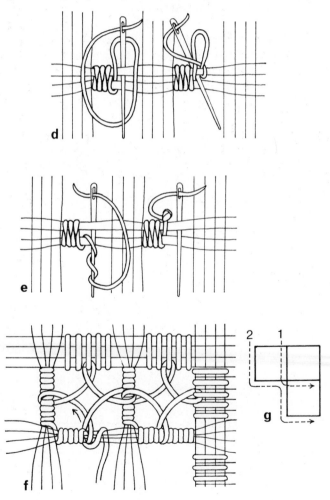

This type of embroidery has traditionally been used mainly on table linen. It can also be most effective on dress, for instance as decoration on a kaftan or some simply shaped garment where the decoration will show to full effect.

3 **Drawn threadwork** is basically an elaboration of hemstitching (see pages 73 and 74), and can be used to form borders or hems of varying widths and complication on any evenly woven material. Once three or more threads have been withdrawn the hemstitching should be worked on both sides of the withdrawn threads forming a small ladder; once six or more threads have been withdrawn some further elaboration is required, and this is called drawn thread embroidery. Although it is an elaboration of hemstitching it need not be worked along a hem. Thread may be withdrawn to form bands of embroidery across a yoke or down the length of a sleeve.

The threads to be withdrawn must be counted and pulled out little

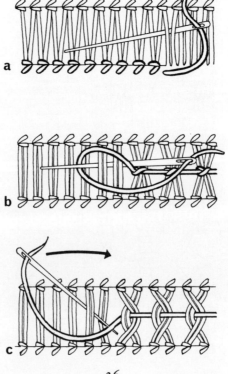

by little along their length with extreme care. The hemstitching is then worked, usually over two or three threads on either side of this border. An alternative is to work the border irregularly, grouping the bundles differently on either side of the border **a**. If the threads have been grouped regularly as a 'ladder', one working thread may be taken down the centre of the ladder, knotting the bundles together two by two with the drawn thread knot **b**. Alternatively, this central single thread may 'single cross' each pair of bundles as in **c**.

Wider composite borders can be built up by grouping bands of these different simple stitches. If more threads are drawn making a wider ladder, the bundles may be knotted in irregular groups by three working threads. If such a border is worked, then a narrow border could be worked on either side, after an interval of solid material, using the 'single cross'.

Where an article with corners is being embroidered in this way, the borders of drawn threads will meet at the corners in a square hole or

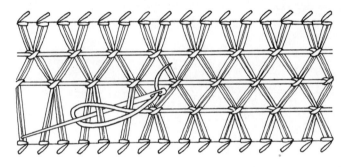

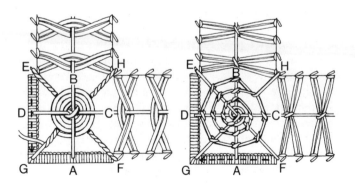

27

space. The threads knotting the bundles in the border can then be thrown across this hole and a woven wheel or spider web wheel be worked on them.

In the same way, more elaborate square or rectangular areas may have some only of the warp and weft threads withdrawn and then the remaining skeleton of threads may be knotted and bunched in a variety of ways. If a square motif is being worked, the edges of the area so to be treated must be finely and invisibly buttonholed first with a thread no thicker than the threads withdrawn. Then the warp threads are carefully counted and withdrawn, or left, as the pattern demands and similarly the weft threads, and are then cut back to the edge of the buttonholing. Since this work is done on a fine closely woven linen the threads must be withdrawn one by one a little at a time. This is the most meticulous part of the work, and requires great care. Then the remaining framework of threads may be worked on by tying the loose threads in bundles and throwing threads across the spaces in criss-cross design. The basic stitch for tying the threads is shown below, and it can be worked not only to form these bundles, but also to create a web in the spaces.

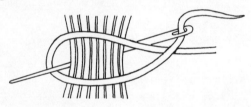

An infinity of elaboration is open to the worker, and not only rectangular but circular patterns can be built up within the cut spaces, sometimes with all the threads, warp and weft, withdrawn. It should be pointed out, however, that the wider and more elaborate the border or motif, the less it will stand up to very hard wear. In fact I have a set of finger bowl mats worked in this style by my great-grandmother which have survived quite considerable use to this day, but they have had a pure silk backing tacked on behind the large motifs of which the mats consist, and this holds the work in shape. Very careful laundering and ironing is essential to avoid tearing the cross threads. The work must be done in a frame (a ring frame is sufficient for this), in order that the new threads thrown across the spaces should not be loose or 'waggly' at all, but only the exact length required to bridge the spaces. Narrow borders have a great potential as a monochrome dress decoration on many modern even weave fabrics.

4 Needleweaving If wide bands of threads are withdrawn one way of the fabric only, these can be replaced by weaving on the remaining threads in a decorative contrasting thread. This is usually a little thicker than the thread of the fabric and is used in a blunt tapestry needle. The work is done in a frame to ensure that the weaving takes the place evenly of the withdrawn threads. A row of 4-sided stitch (see p. 43) may be worked (but not pulled tight) along each of the long sides of the band to be worked on before drawing the threads. This facilitates working and neatens the finish of the border. Where wide bands are withdrawn, these threads are not cut off but are darned back into the material **a**. This is possible as the fabric used is not usually of the most closely woven type. The ends of the bands are overcast, buttonholed or satin stitched over the darned in ends.

The threads remaining may then be grouped in twos by hemstitching, or in threes by four-sided stitch worked along the length. The work is then ready for weaving on—over one group and under a second and back. Traditionally this has been done in regular geometric shapes, usually in fairly small units increasing and decreasing in steps **b**. Sometimes the threads are completely covered by the weaving, but sometimes small areas are left uncovered; sometimes the weaving is done in such a way that spaces are left between the woven groups— spaces as important in themselves as the solid weaving. The thread is begun and ended by being slipped into the bands of weaving **c**.

In traditional needleweaving part of the skill lies in the even, regular tension of the weaving, taking care as work is in progress not to pull the bands of weaving askew, and out of the vertical. In modern needleweaving, however, the fashion is rather for irregularity. This irregularity may be reflected in an asymmetric design on the withdrawn border, but also an irregular pattern may be woven by pulling the threads more or less tightly thus leaving negative shapes between the woven areas.

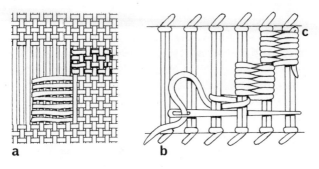

a   b

Needleweaving can also be worked as free embroidery not restricted to the counted threads. Threads are thrown over the surface of the background material and the weaving is worked on them. The essence is still in the in-and-out weaving on base threads, but the weaving is not an integral part of the fabric. These base threads may be placed in a regular and parallel pattern, or irregularly and not parallel to each other, but the basic method of over and under weaving (so similar to darning!) is the same. All kinds of threads may be used for this surface needleweaving; indeed since much of the interest lies in the contrasting textures of the work, unusual threads and wools, padded areas and beads may all be incorporated.

Traditional needleweaving often employed stitches such as satin stitch and herringbone in order to blend the solid woven areas into the background of the material. Similarly modern needleweaving also uses other surface stitchery to avoid monotony and give tone and depth.

(For stitches see section on Stitches, page 50.)

5 Richelieu embroidery Cut work embroidery differs from drawn thread in that instead of some threads only being carefully withdrawn, leaving others to form a basis for the decoration, whole areas are cut away either to emphasize what has been left, or to build up a new decorative stitchery in the spaces. In past times there were several degrees of elaboration of cut work all of which bore different names, but in the interests of simplification I have included two only.

Richelieu work consists of designs outlined in buttonhole stitch with the spaces between the units of the design cut away. A fairly simple flower border will naturally have small spaces between the flowers, and between the flowers and leaves. When all the leaves and flowers have been outlined in buttonhole stitch, these little interstices are cut away very carefully with fine pointed scissors and without damaging the buttonholing. In some cases these spaces are bridged by little bars, buttonholed or overcast, and there may be small ladder-like strips, or curved strips, outside the design which help to blend it into the body of the cloth. Nowadays commercial designs are widely available which have simplified the traditional Richelieu work by omitting all the little bars. This is a pity as they break up the 'solid' areas of space and give a lighter and daintier texture to the work.

The work is done on a firm close linen with not too thick a thread, but possibly one with a contrasting sheen to the fabric, and a crewel needle is used. The design is first worked throughout in one, or better still two, lines of small even running stitch on the edge and 2 or 3 mm

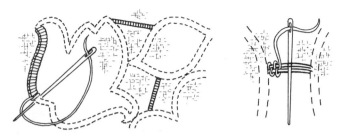

($\frac{1}{8}$") in from the edge. If there are bars to be worked, they are worked at this stage. When working the running stitch throw a thread across, or across and back, over a projected space to another section of outline. Then work across the thread bar in buttonhole or overcasting. Continue the running stitch from there. If the gap is rather large, four or six threads can be thrown across and a tiny needleweaving bar be worked. When the running stitch and all the bars are completed the buttonholed edging is worked over the two lines of running—very close and very even, with the purl edge to the outside, where the space will be. Only when this is complete, cut away the spaces.

Further variety can be made by adding little picots to the buttonholed bars **a**. For these either a pin for a simple loop picot, or a holding thread for a buttonholed picot **b** and **c**, are a help to keep the picot in

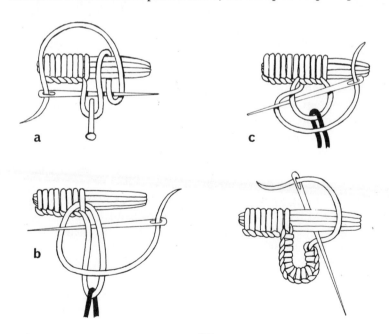

place till the bar is completed. Three-way bars **d** may be made to bridge an inconvenient three-cornered space. Work half the bar **A** to **B**, then throw one thread over to **C**; work back to centre, then complete to **B**.

Spider bars will bridge an unusually large space **e**. Work one thread across the space **A-B** and overcast it back to start **A**. With small running stitches work round to **C** and proceed to work a second leg **C-D** and overcast back to **C**. The last leg **E-F** is only overcast to the centre. Then weave under and over the legs at the central crossing going round twice. Complete by overcasting the last leg to the edge **E**.

The work is usually finished by a scalloped buttonholed edge, which may be padded by using more than the two rows of running stitch.

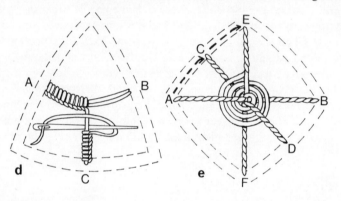

6 **Reticella work** differs from the last in that it has an entirely new fabric built up with the needle in the cut spaces. The spaces are therefore important as containers for the stitchery, not as above as a frame for the design. It is also worked on a firmly woven fine linen with linen or strong cotton threads. The linen is made ready for working by having the space to be cut outlined very carefully in running stitch. Then the area to be cut away is slashed from the centre to the corners and the flaps of material are turned under to the running stitch line and this double edge overcast, or sometimes buttonholed neatly and regularly, but not as closely as in Richelieu work **a** (opposite). Cut away the surplus flaps on the back.

When the hole has been prepared the work needs to be tacked onto a backing such as calico or waxed mapping paper, and then mounted in a frame so that the new areas of stitchery will not be 'floppy' in their spaces. Now a design of geometric patterns can be built up. Threads are thrown across the space and overcast or woven; on these crossing bars semicircular motifs can be built up. For this part of the work a fine tapestry needle can best ensure that the threads are not split accidentally nor the backing sewn into. The first row from the centre is a row of little buttonholed bars with picots worked as in Richelieu work **b**. Care must be taken to let the threads thrown round 'sag' a bit in order to achieve the circular effect on the set of four.

The next row is a buttonholed segment. First throw a thread across to the next dissecting bar, remembering to let it 'sag' into a nice quarter circle. Then work across from left to right one row of buttonhole. Return, oversewing into the base of the buttonholes just worked. Work another buttonhole row from left to right, missing out the first and last stitches to give the decreasing shape **c**. The final stitch of the segment is attached to the corner or other chosen point of the

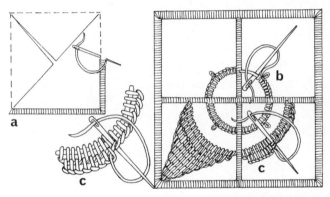

a

b

c

c

design. The thread may be finished off by carefully running it into the back of the worked stitches. Areas of this type of work may be blended into the plain part of the work with satin stitch or four-sided stitch borders.

An infinite variety of shapes and patterns can be built up, giving the traditional rich and lace-like embroidery that we so admire on dress and furnishings, particularly ecclesiastical furnishings of the sixteenth and seventeenth centuries.

Metal thread embroidery

The use of gold and silver threads for embroidery was at one time confined to ecclesiastical and other regalia, and to ceremonial robes and trappings. Nowadays it is widely used for panels and boxes as well as small articles for evening use. The increase in the numbers of

33

synthetic threads, cords, leathers, braids and beads has added to the variety of effects and textures possible to the embroideress.

Metal threads are generally applied to the surface of the fabric using couching techniques, although a few of the synthetic threads may be threaded in a needle and used through the material. In couching, the main thread, or more frequently two threads side by side treated as one, is laid on the surface of the background fabric on the line or curve of the design and then held in that position by tiny stitches over it. These stitches arranged 'brick' fashion in each row may be as inconspicuous as possible in matching silk thread, or may be designed as a contrast in a coloured silk thread over spaced laid threads.

Traditionally couched threads were laid as close to each other as possible, completely filling that part of the design area. Nowadays there is more consciousness of the part played by the 'non-embroidered' spaces in a design, and the couched work may only partly fill the design area. The couching need not necessarily be flat but may be looped, knotted or twisted and spiralled, and laid at opposing angles in order to achieve the maximum play of light on which the embroidery depends for effect.

These laid metal threads are taken through the material only at the beginning and end of their length. To start couching, the two strands of metal thread are laid on the surface of the background in the desired position with surplus 'tails' of 2–4 cm (1″–2″) at the start of the line of stitching. These strands are held in position while a needle threaded with maltese silk in gold or silver as appropriate is used to couch them down. This couching thread must be beeswaxed for strength down its whole length before sewing with it. A small stitch is taken over these metal strands to hold them down. Repeat this first stitch to secure them firmly. Bring the needle up 0·5 cm (¼″) along the line of the metal strands and take another stitch over them.

When a whole length of metal strands has been sewn down, cut them off with the tails of 2–4 cm (1″–2″). These tails may be taken through the material and lightly sewn down on the wrong side straight away or at a later stage. This may be done by threading the tail in a

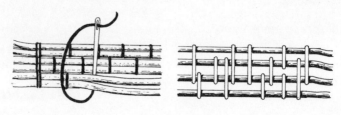

34

coarse-eyed sharp-pointed chenille needle and pulling it through to the back, or by making a hole with a stiletto and threading the metal thread through that hole. Obviously the finer and firmer the fabric the more tricky this is to do without making too large a hole in the fabric which cannot then be concealed under other threads.

The most used threads are very fine gold or silver rolled around a silk core, and these may be real gold or silver, or imitation; twist, which comes in several thicknesses and is three metal threads twisted to give a much rougher textured thread than the above; purls and checks, which are very fine wires coiled in differing ways. These last can be cut and threaded on the needle-like beads, or couched on the surface. The modern worker may also use cog wheels and springs and other metal parts from watches, machinery and even cars, as well as glass and stones where they contribute to the desired effect and are not merely gimmicky. The use of a padding of string (as in basket stitch shown at **a** and **b** below), felt or card adds to the effect of depth and texture, and the combination of metal threads with other silks or threads can contribute to the harmony of the work and prevent the vulgarity of over richness.

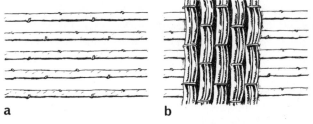

a   **b**

The work must be done in a frame with the material carefully tacked to a washed calico or cotton backing. A rectangular frame must be used and the material mounted very taut and with the extra row of tacking as described in the introduction (page 5). The manipulation of the threads may take a little time to master, particularly the taking of the ends of the metal threads through the fabric. As with all embroidery, practice can rapidly make perfect and the beauty of the threads and the thrilling result of their application to a well-conceived design are their own reward.

In times past metal threads were more narrowly used according to a fairly rigid code, but nowadays in this medium as in others, the embroideress may experiment with methods and threads, and with combinations of method and thread, a meaningful or beautiful result being the only criterion of rightness.

Patchwork

This is an age-old craft beloved for its bright and striking effects by home-loving women through the centuries. There is an inherent fascination in piecing together gaily coloured fragments into simple or intricate designs which are never likely to lose their charm. The simplicity of the work however is deceptive, because a great deal of the resultant charm lies in the degree of care and taste with which the colour and layout of the patchwork is planned. A beautifully worked piece of patchwork may fail in its impact if the tone weight of the colours and the balance of the patterned and plain materials is not well judged. For this reason it is best to consider the article to be made very carefully and to sketch out the design in rough, and perhaps even work it out in toned paper so that the relative lights and darks can be considered. The size and shape of the patches must also be considered in relation to the size of the article being made, for an intricate fussy design may not be ideal for a bedspread, nor a design in large units for a tea cosy.

The fabrics to be used should be considered together with the overall design. Cotton, or cotton blends must always be favourites, although other fabrics may be used. The overriding consideration must be only to combine materials of the same type and weight, and with the same washing or cleaning characteristics. It is not advisable to use fabric from old dresses for patchwork. It is in any case surprising how quickly new cotton fabrics fade and rot in today's big-windowed sunlit houses, and if already partly worn material is used, the hours of work will not reap their due reward in length of service.

There are innumerable traditional shapes for patchwork, but probably the most enduringly popular is the hexagon. This one shape can be used to form rosettes and stripes **a**, and in combination with diamonds **b**, stars as well. Diamonds alone can make the strikingly 'modern' box design **c** with its three-dimensional effect; another traditional arrangement is the Dutch tile pattern **d** made up of small squares with large octagons. There are many books available on the history of patchwork which give illustrations of the innumerable designs used by the patchwork quilt makers of the past—and in this craft America was surely pre-eminent.

Templates of the chosen shapes are required from which to cut the patches. These can be bought in quite a variety of shapes and sizes, but they are not necessarily any more accurate than a template made at home in hardboard or some other enduring material which will not be

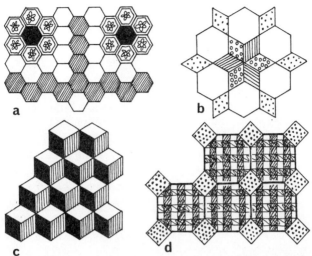

a

b

c

d

spoiled by use. From the template cut a number of the patch shapes in thin card—the backs of old Christmas cards are admirable for this purpose. Remember that the angle at which the pencil is held when drawing round the template can make considerable difference to the accuracy of your patch. This is not fussiness. If the patches are not accurately cut they will not fit together well and the work will be uneven and lumpy. As well, cut one 'window' or 'negative' patch of the chosen shape. This is most useful when a patch is being cut from a patterned material as it enables the worker to isolate the most suitable pattern motif for her patch.

Then cut the fabric patches, remembering to cut them 0·5 cm ($\frac{1}{4}''$) larger each way than the template, to allow for turnings. If a thick material is used larger turning allowance may be required. At this stage care should be taken with the placing of the templates on the material. The straight grain of the material should lie with one of the straight sides of the patch. If this is not done the patches can pull out of shape and stretch and pucker more easily. All the patches should lie

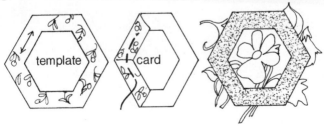

template   card

the same way in the finished article, but particularly with a background fabric, the play of light can be rather pleasant and less monotonous if the patches are placed with the grain *not* all lying the same way. Take a patch, lay the card shape carefully on it, remembering to lay one side along the grain. Turn the surplus edges over and tack them down with firm stitches, two or more to each side depending on the size. I always turn over the side lying along the grain first to ensure it is straight. At this point it should be mentioned that one school of thought says that this tacking should not penetrate through to the right side of the patch as this will invariably mark the fabric. This school tacks the turning only onto itself taking a back stitch at the corners to secure them. When the patchwork is of silk this is obviously wise, but may not always be necessary or possible with springy materials. Make up a good many patches and arrange them in the chosen design to check on the best layout before sewing together.

Sewing should be done with as fine a Sharp needle and as fine sewing cotton as the worker can manage, or can obtain! Drima is now also widely used. White cotton is used on multicoloured articles and the stitches should be so small as not to show on the right side. Place the two patches to be sewn together, right sides together, and starting with a double oversewing stitch, oversew the edges of one side together. Then open these two patches up and place another facing the next side to be sewn. Care must be taken at corners and points so that a little hole does not appear on the right side. After the work is finished take out the tacking and the card shapes will come out with a little tweak. If the stitches are small enough they are not likely to have sewn through the card in many places.

Patchwork is usually lined because it needs the raw edges on the back covered, but it may instead be applied to a background material. Patchwork has traditionally been used for bedcovers and cushions, but is today increasingly used for boxes and bags, and as a decoration on dress.

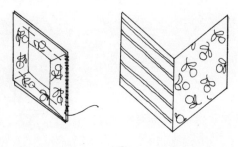

Pulled linen embroidery

This kind of work is often confused with drawn threadwork, but in reality there is very little similarity except that traditionally both are done on linen in self colour, and that both are commonly used for table linen. In this work the linen, or other even weave material used, must be comparatively loosely woven so that the threads can be bunched together without puckering. A thread of the same thickness as the thread of the material is used in a tapestry needle so as not to split the threads of the fabric. Patterns are created by working the stitches over precisely counted numbers of threads, and by pulling these stitches tight differing arrangements of pattern bunches are formed. In combination with satin stitches in a thicker, glossier thread, fascinating variations in texture, light and lacy or more dense and rich, can be achieved. Because of the nature of the embroidery the original material is made stronger by the stitching rather than weakened, and the result is a very durable type of decoration for all table linen. This is not the only use of this work today, however. It has been used delightfully on lampshades, the light showing through the pattern of little pulled holes, and as a form of decoration on even weave fabrics for dress.

Traditional designs for pulled work were fairly simple and bold in order to give a sufficient area of one stitch for the texture to have its full effect. These areas would be outlined with whipped chain, or stem stitch, all in self colour. As the stitches are worked by counting the threads horizontally, vertically, or on the diagonal, geometric designs make the finishing of the rows less ragged, and are easier for a beginner to negotiate. Nowadays the popularity of abstract designs obtains in this technique as in so many others, and patterns are created to show off the textural effects of the stitches. The areas of stitching are not necessarily outlined, although the balance of design still requires thin and more solid lines to be worked in to add variety to the textural areas.

As the name implies the effects are obtained by working geometric stitches at differing tensions. For this reason it is not usually necessary to work in a frame as this will probably prevent the necessary pull being exercised. Some of these stitches are comparatively simple, some more intricate. Satin stitch can be worked as a contrast without 'pull', but satin stitch itself can be used as a pulled stitch when worked in a thread equivalent to that of the fabric. The varying degree of tension in successive stitches will create a simple pattern.

The satin stitch is worked here over 4 threads, but is pulled in the centre to the width of two **a**. Obviously there is an infinity of variations possible in the arrangement of the satin stitch. Worked at an angle to itself the play of light on it will increase the degree of variation. A very popular arrangement of satin stitch is called eyelet stitch which may be pulled more, or less, tight depending on the effect required **b**.

Regular shaped eyelets have always been popular, contrasting as they do a pronounced hole with the thick area of stitch surrounding it. Today irregular eyelets are equally popular. These are worked with the hole off centre and with the surrounding converging stitches of differing lengths on one side of the hole to those on the other **c**. Frequently not all the surround is worked.

In addition to stitches based on satin stitch, there are stitches based on back stitch, again arranged in varying ways to give varying results. One of these variations is festoon stitch, in which the simple back stitch is worked in a festoon shape but each stitch is pulled tight **d**.

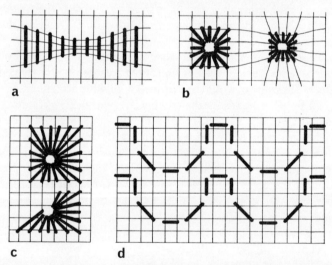

a   b

c   d

The best results in this kind of embroidery are often obtained by sticking to relatively few stitches in any one piece of work. The embroideress can most usefully keep a piece of her linen for trying out her stitches before finally choosing which to use as no picture in a book can give a true impression of the final effect of the more intricate stitches. It must also be remembered that by altering the number of threads over which the stitch is worked and thus altering the scale of the stitch, its effect in relation to neighbouring stitches may be varied again.

Some other pulled linen stitches are shown on page 40.

Wave stitch filling This is worked from right to left. The needle comes through from the back at the start and goes in four threads down and two to the right; passing behind, it comes out four threads to the left. The needle goes in again at the start and, passing behind, it comes out four to the left and goes in again four down and two to the right. Continue. The next row, upside down to the first, thus completes a diamond pattern, which gives alternate rows of holes.

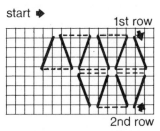

Window filling Worked from right to left it resembles wave stitch filling except that a vertical thread is left between each stitch and a horizontal thread is left between each row. The needle comes out at the start and goes in four threads down and two to the right. Passing behind, it comes out *five* threads to the left. The needle goes in again four threads up and two to the right. Continue the row. The second row is worked one thread below the bottom of the first pattern and upside down to it. Thus a little cross is left between the rows of holes like a child's drawing of a window.

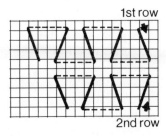

Honeycomb filling This stitch is worked towards the worker. The needle comes out at the start and goes in three threads to the right. It comes out three threads down; in three threads up again and out three

41

threads below; in three threads to the left and out three threads down; in three threads up again and out three threads below. The second row is worked in the same way, but back to front, repeating the vertical stitches where the rows touch.

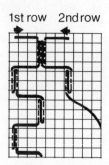

Single faggot stitch This is worked diagonally from top right to bottom left. Bring the needle out at the start and insert it four threads up. Bring it out four threads down and four to the left. Go in at the start and come out four threads down and four threads to the left. Continue. The second row is worked on top of the first and completes the squares. This second row can be worked by turning the work round.

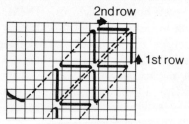

Cushion stitch This stitch is worked from right to left. The needle comes out at the start and goes in two threads to the right; it comes out two threads down and two to the left. The second stitch goes in two threads to the right and comes out four threads up and four to the left; then in two threads to the right and out six threads down and two to the left. In the second row count carefully so that the three stitches at the base of the cushion are repeated as the top of the second row of cushions. As will be seen, this is a form of back stitch with a great deal more 'stitch' on the back. Pulled tight, this does form a cushion outlined by tiny holes on the right side—the shared hole tending to be larger.

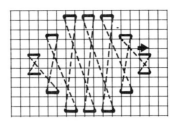

Four-sided stitch This is worked from right to left, and may be pulled more or less according to required result. It may be used as a filling or a border. The stitch may be worked over two or four threads. It is worked in the order shown in the diagram.

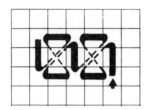

Quilting

Quilting is a technique which may mean different things to different people as it covers three quite distinct variations under the same name: English or padded quilting, Italian or corded quilting, and Trapunto or stuffed quilting. All three styles are essentially padded embroidery, but the methods of achieving the raised areas are rather different. Naturally since all quilting is padded, it is a technique which lends itself to use on bed covers, cushions or warm, loose outer layers of dress. Traditionally in this country it has mainly been used for bed quilts, and fine old designs are still handed down in some parts of the north-east and Wales. Today however in the search for an up-to-date use which, we must confess, will not take quite as many hours of labour, quilting can be used on jerkins and bed-jackets, and as a decoration on boxes and bags.

1 **English quilting** is worked through three layers of materials: a top layer which may be silk, fine cotton or fine linen; a centre layer of, traditionally, carded lamb's wool, though domette or flannel may be used; and a lining layer which may be the same as the top layer or may be a fine linen. The work is always done in a square frame, though not stretched very tight, and before mounting great care must be taken to

43

tack the work across and across, horizontally and vertically by the grain of the fabric, creating a trellis 8–16 cm (3″–6″) square. This may seem laborious but it is essential if the three materials are not to slip askew in working. Traditional designs were often built up on such commonplace objects as a feather, wine glass, heart or shell, often with some parts of the background left plain, and some parts more closely worked over in diamond quilting. The thread used should as closely resemble the thread of the material as possible, and is in self colour or only a tone or two deeper. Naturally there is no need today to stick to this tradition, but somehow English quilting is one of those techniques which shows to greatest advantage in one neutral colour. Our ancestors did sometimes know best! The stitch used is running or back stitch, with sometimes a little chain stitch, and the perfect evenness of the stitching is one of the features of the work. This kind of quilting can very well be used on the fashionable long waistcoats or jerkins of today.

2 **Italian quilting** is worked through two layers of material: a top layer of silk or satin, or some other fabric with a pronounced sheen; and a lining layer of butter muslin. The designs for this kind of quilting need to have some continuous flow with as few breaks as possible about them. The outlines of the design are drawn throughout as double lines for the later insertion of a soft padding cord. The work is done on the back in neat running stitches through both layers; therefore the design needs to be transferred onto the muslin and not onto the right side of the silk. The two layers must be well tacked together before starting work, but the stitching need not be done in a frame. When threading the soft padding cord through the channels between the silk and the muslin take care at all corners or junctions to bring the cord out through the muslin and to leave loops before re-entering the same hole again and continuing threading. This will allow for pulling and shrinking. The cord can be held in position on the back at the beginning and ending by a few stitches through the muslin backing. In the fairly rare cases where a wider area has to be filled with padding, the cord can be taken out of the muslin, leaving a loop, then over a thread and back through the space again and across it as many times as required until it is filled.

3 **Trapunto quilting** is used in combination with surface stitching where small padded areas are desired for contrast. Again it is worked through two layers of material: silk and a muslin backing, but a cord

padding is not used and so the design units need not be worked out with double lines. In fact the padded areas must be entirely self-contained and independent, as each is padded separately. The outlines are worked in back stitch in a pure silk thread, and it is advisable to work in a ring frame. After completion a small hole is made in the muslin backing and small pieces of cotton wadding are pushed and pulled through into the outlined area with a steel crochet hook. Some skill is required to pad these areas evenly so that they are neither too fat nor too flat! Other stitchery and beads may be used on the right side to enhance the effect of the raised area. Such treatment makes this kind of quilting ideal for use on small decorative articles such as bags and boxes.

A variation of this type of quilting is shadow quilting where the top layer is of organdie. Coloured fragments of thread and fabric are inserted from behind as in normal Trapunto quilting and they show through their colour muted by the surface fabric. Subtle and delicate effects can thus be achieved.

Smocking

This is a traditional form of dress decoration which, from having been at one time the peculiar dress of a certain class of farm worker, has spread to ornament the dress of young children and, at varying times according to fashion, of women's dress too. It is in fact a method of dealing with the fullness in the body of a smock before it is attached to the yoke of the garment, but it can of course be used to decorate any extremely full garment, or part of a garment. So sleeve tops, sleeves at the cuffs, blouses into yokes, skirts into waistbands, may all be smocked. Panels of smocking may be inset purely for decoration into the bib front of dress or to form pockets. Nowadays experiments with a wider use of smocking are being carried out. It has been used to decorate cushions, and the technique has been tried with varying success on lampshades and bags, and in combination with other embroidery applied to panels.

A great variety of materials can be used for smocking—any fabric in fact which the worker finds not too coarse to handle. Traditional workers' smocks were for outdoor work and were of correspondingly stout material. Nowadays a reasonably fine fabric is preferred: silk, fine woollens, cotton and linen. The stitching is worked in a stranded or twisted cotton or silk thread, the thickness of which must vary according to the material worked; this is of considerable importance to the finished effect. Too few strands, or too thin a thread, will give a spidery insignificant appearance, while too thick a thread will look heavy and coarse. Experience, and trial and error alone can determine this.

Three times the amount of material should be allowed to the final width of the smocking. Rows of gauging precisely under each other must be worked across the material to the depth the smocking is required. Commercial transfers of smocking dots in various sizes can be bought to facilitate perfectly even gauging. The horizontal distance apart of the dots regulates the depth of the pleats and the finer the fabric the closer the dots need to be. These dots can be ironed off onto the material of the garment. Care must be taken when placing them on the material that the rows of dots run accurately straight across the grain of the material. They should never be ironed onto the right side of the fabric as most of these transfer inks do not wash off easily. On a very fine or semi-transparent material it is better not to iron them onto the material at all, but to tack the sheet of dots onto the wrong side of the fabric and stitch through the paper, pulling it off when the dots

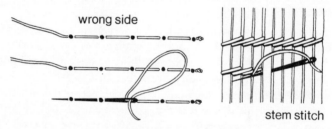

wrong side

stem stitch

have all been worked. Naturally on a printed or woven fabric with checks or stripes it is possible to work without dots. The gauging is worked from the back, and can be started with a knot and a back stitch. It is essential that one long thread should complete a whole row across the work leaving the end loose to pull up. When all the rows have been worked—usually to a depth of no less than 4–6 cm ($1\frac{1}{2}''$–$2''$) the gauging threads may be pulled up. It is a good idea to pull them all up gently to their greatest tightness at first and to leave them pulled up overnight to ensure a slight natural crease in them, before relaxing the threads to the measurement the smocking is finally to take. The ends may then be knotted together in pairs, or groups, or twisted round a pin or pins. At this stage stroke the gathers carefully and ensure the even distribution of the fullness across the width before starting the stitching.

It is advisable to start the rows of stitching at the top with a stitch which will firmly control the fullness. For this two rows of stem, or outline, stitch are ideal. The embroideress works the stem stitch from left to right across the top surface of the pleats just picking up the top of each pleat.

Other variations are shown below. Experience will show the worker which stitches give a greater and which a lesser degree of elasticity. Individual workers will also find that they work to a different personal tension which they will learn to allow for.

Traditional smocks were worked on plain material, but they can be very successful on patterned fabrics as well, although this may make the choice of colours for the stitching more difficult. Some workers prefer to work in one colour or shades of one colour, but this is a matter of taste and by no means compulsory, although perhaps caution is advisable at first. When the stitching is finished the gauging

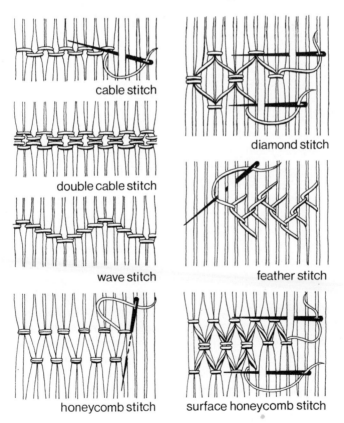

cable stitch

double cable stitch

wave stitch

honeycomb stitch

diamond stitch

feather stitch

surface honeycomb stitch

47

threads are withdrawn carefully and the work can be attached to the rest of the garment.

The best method of securing the gathered fullness of a very full skirt or nightdress into the other part of the garment is to hem it by hand. The straight part of the garment, bodice or yoke, should have the seam allowance folded under and be pinned over the gathers, the gathers having been carefully and equally distributed along the length they are to take up. The bodice or yoke is then hemmed to the full part, each hemming stitch going through one gather. The wrong side should then be worked in the same way, although it is satisfactory for all practical purposes if the turnings are machined together on the back 3 mm ($\frac{3}{8}''$) inside the hemming. The work should be pressed only very, very lightly on the back.

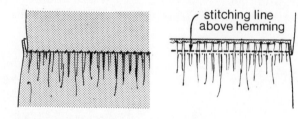

Shadow work

This kind of embroidery is worked in fine thread on transparent or semi-transparent fabrics such as organdie, or very fine silk or lawn. It has usually been worked in white on white, but individual workers may prefer to use colours. It should then be remembered, however, that although the body of the stitching will show through the fabric suitably pastel, the double running stitches which outline the design are in their full colour. Therefore only the palest of shades is really appropriate if the contrast between the delicate stitchery and the colour used is not to spoil the whole conception.

The main stitch, almost the only stitch, used is herringbone worked closely on the wrong side, or if the worker prefers, double back stitch worked closely on the right side. The herringbone stitches are worked right across the design and show through the fabric on the right side as a density of white or a shadow, the threads only barely perceptibly separable from each other. These shadow motifs show as outlined in tiny back stitches. Because of this method of working the design needs to be very carefully balanced. Wide areas or motifs are not suitable as if the herringbone stitches are too long they are liable to catch; but too thin and weedy a design is not desirable either. In some cases a wider motif can be worked in several rows of herringbone, filling the space in stages.

A little surface stitchery is sometimes used with the herringbone to give variety. Some pulled four-sided stitch may be used as a filling, and sometimes a line stitch such as chain or stem stitch. Additional depth can be given by applying areas of the background fabric—say organdie—on the back and working over it. Afterwards the surplus may be trimmed away. In this way three different layers of density may be achieved.

This kind of work is particularly suitable for delicate feminine wear and dainty articles. Bridal veils and christening robes are obviously suitable, and afternoon tea cloths, tray cloths and tea cosies, where such refinements are still in use, in place of the more mundane gingham! It is also attractive on lampshades because of its transparent quality.

Stitches

Stitches which are used almost exclusively in one particular technique have been dealt with in the appropriate section, but this leaves other stitches which may be used in various techniques. These may be classed according to their uses: as outlines or as fillings, for shading or for borders, or for spot decoration. Of course some stitches fall under several headings so I have included as many of the most useful and attractive stitches as I can, in alphabetical order.

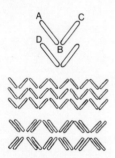

Arrowhead stitch is useful as a filling or as a border or line stitch. The stitch may be worked slightly open at the bottom or closed. The needle comes out at **A** and enters the material again at **B**, out at **C** and in again at **B** or a thread or two to the right. The next stitch is made directly below the first, the thread coming out at **D**.

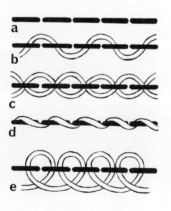

Back stitch is basically a plain sewing stitch which may also be used as an embroidery line stitch worked from right to left **a**. The needle is brought out a few threads along the line, re-inserted at the start of the stitch, and brought out a stitch-length ahead of the previous stitch. It can be elaborated by *threading* it with a contrasting thread **b**, by double threading it **c**, possibly in two colours, whipping **d**, or it can be threaded with a backwards loop, when it is called *pekinese* stitch **e**.

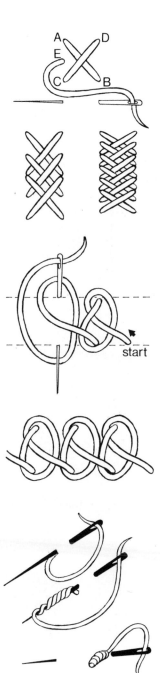

Basket stitch This stitch can be worked closely or more openly, and forms a solid line or border, or a filling for small shapes such as leaves.

Braid stitch This stitch makes an attractive wide line or border. The thread loop has to be held down with the left thumb while pulling the needle through.

Bullion knot forms little separate ropelike twists of thread. Worked close together they make a filling. Twist the thread six or seven times round the needle.

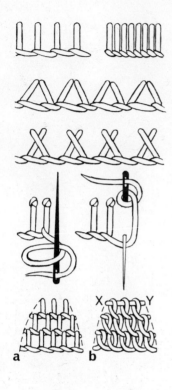

Buttonhole stitch is described on pages 75 and 76. The only difference between this stitch and blanket stitch lies in the spacing between the stitches. In blanket stitch the stitches are worked further apart than in buttonhole, where they are worked close, or very close, together. The difference is shown above. Other variations follow.

Worked as a *filling* it can be shaded in rows. It can be worked into the background material in the normal way **a**, or on the surface only **b**. Work from left to right into the loops of the row before and take the needle through the material only at the beginning and end of the row, when it passes behind and comes out at the left-hand side again. A few running stitches may be taken from **x-y** to start 'looping' into.

Chain stitch This stitch is worked more easily in the hand than in a frame, though care must be taken not to pucker the work by pulling the stitches too tight. It is best worked towards the worker with the loop held down by the left hand while the needle is being placed and pulled through. A good tension will produce nicely rounded chains. The point of the needle goes back at the same point that it came out.

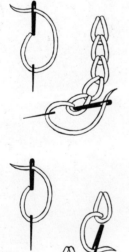

Detached chain is worked in the same way as continuous chain except that once the needle has come up through the chain loop it re-enters the material on the other side of this loop thus holding it down.

Whipped chain This is a fine line stitch which makes a more raised line than chain. Having worked a line of chain stitch and using a matching or contrasting thread, overcast into each stitch but do not enter the material except at the beginning and end. Other variations are: *back-stitched chain*, the back-stitching worked up the centre of the chain.

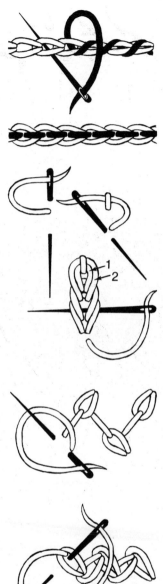

Heavy chain Starting with a running stitch, the first two stitches slip under this. Thereafter the needle passes under the two previous chains, not taking up any material, and re-enters the fabric at the point at which it came out, re-emerging a little below for the next stitch.

Feathered chain makes a pleasant border stitch. This stitch has an outsize 'anchor' stitch taking the stitch at a slant across to a parallel line for the next chain.

Zig-zag chain Each stitch is worked at an angle to the last.

Double threaded chain consists of detached chain stitches in a line threaded through from both sides.

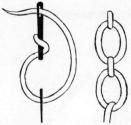

Cable chain stitch When working this stitch the thread must be held down while the needle passes over it to make the link between the chains.

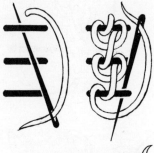

Raised chain band makes a most charming raised border stitch. It is worked in two parts. First a ladder of horizontal threads equally spaced is worked. Then the chain is worked on this ladder with the needle never penetrating the material except at the beginning and end.

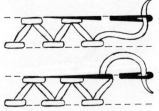

Chevron stitch is an attractive simple border stitch.

Coral stitch is a useful line stitch. The thread loop must be held down with the left thumb while the stitch is made. This can also be worked zig-zag.

Couching This has been described in relation to metal threads on page 34.

A thread of one colour or thickness is laid on the surface of the material and sewn down with thread of a different colour. The stitches which are used to sew the couched thread down are so arranged as to form part of the decoration. The couched threads are usually arranged in a trellis formation, and some spot stitch is often worked in the centre of the squares so formed.

couching held down by contrasting cross stitch

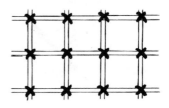

couching held down with half cross stitch and decorated with french knots

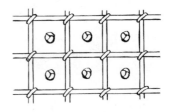

couching in two different shades held down by tiny stitches of matching colours

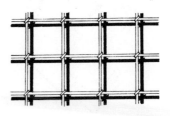

couching held down with cross stitch and decorated with detached chain

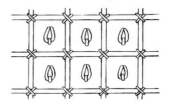

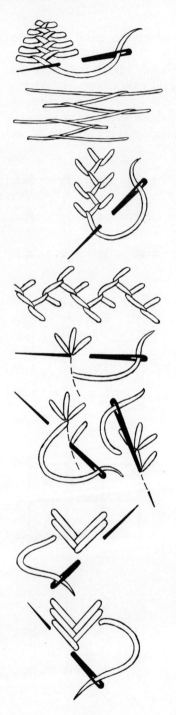

Cretan stitch is a very popular stitch worked open, or closed, regularly or irregularly.

Feather stitch is a related stitch to the last, worked first to one side then the other. In a common variation used in smocking, three stitches are taken in each direction.

Fern stitch is a simple straight line stitch useful in floral embroidery.

Fishbone stitch is another stitch that can be worked open or closed. The stitches slightly overlap in the centre.

Fly stitch may be worked as a line stitch for borders, detached as a spot stitch, or in lines as a filling stitch, in which case the second row is worked upside down to the first row. The length of the holding stitch can be varied according to need.

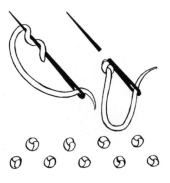

French knots are little separate raised knots. They can be used as spot decoration or as a closely worked filling. The needle is brought out from the back and the thread is wound twice round the needle and re-inserted next to the point at which the thread came out. The twists need to be held with the left hand while the thread is pulled through or an unpleasing loop may result instead of the knot. If they are worked as a filling, for instance to fill an acorn cup, the needle can take up a thread or two of material close to the last knot and have the thread twisted round it in that position.

Herringbone stitch This stitch is useful both in plain sewing and embroidery. The length of the stitches can be varied to make an interesting pattern. It may be *threaded* in another colour. *Double herringbone* is worked in alternate colours.

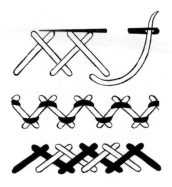

Lazy daisy stitch is really a detached chain stitch worked with rather a long chain to resemble a petal. It is included under this name as it is one stitch that everyone knows!

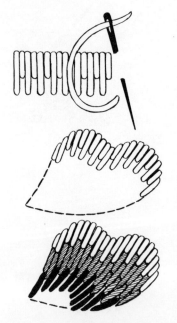

Long and short stitch This stitch is an arrangement of satin stitch which is widely used for delicate shading for flowers, birds or human faces. The working of the first row of stitches gives this stitch its name. The first row consists of alternate long and short straight stitches next to each other. A full length stitch is worked on the back.

In the second row and succeeding rows the stitches are all the same length. The second row is worked on top of the short stitches of the first row; the third row is worked on the long stitches of the first row. Thus the step pattern is retained in working. Its excellence for shading lies in the fact that the overlapping and interlocking rows of stitches do not give a hard line. The direction of the stitch may be gradually altered to allow for the developing shape of a flower petal. More stitches can be added or left out in the pattern to allow for increase or decrease in the size of motif. The shading need not be consistent along a row thus allowing a petal to have for example dark borders.

A line of running stitch or back stitch should first be worked along the edge of the petal or leaf, then worked over by the first line of stitches.

Overcast stitch makes a narrow raised line stitch. The overcasting is worked on a base of running stitch. The overcasting is worked over this with the needle picking up the smallest amount of material.

Or it may be worked over stem stitch with the needle slipping through between the stitches and the material without entering the material.

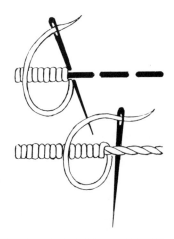

Pinstitch is particularly useful for a fine decorative finish not necessarily on the grain, or straight thread, of the material. It can also be used for appliqué, setting on lace, seams or tucks. It is used on lingerie, and such fine garments as christening robes. The method is as for hemstitching (page 73) except that no weft threads are withdrawn.

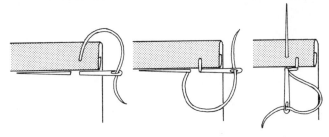

Instead a few threads of solid material are picked up on the needle, and in order to increase the decorative effect of the tiny holes a rather thicker needle is used than might be expected and the stitches are pulled tight. The diagram below shows how the stitch can be used in joining two pieces of fabric.

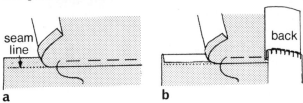

seam
line

back

a   b

When used for appliqué the stitching is worked on the right side. The piece of material to be applied is tacked on with a very tiny fold turned under. It will help the worker if the tacking stitches are withdrawn stitch by stitch just in advance of the pinstitching.

Punchstitch   This is a stitch used in fine sewing as an alternative to pinstitch for seams, hems and for attaching lace. It can also be used for appliqué, especially on fine lingerie and net. The effect of a double row of tiny holes is obtained in one journey. A fine thread is used and the stitches are pulled tight to form little holes. As with pinstitching a thicker needle than might be expected may be used to make the holes more pronounced. The stitch is worked from right to left. It need not be worked along the thread of the fabric, but can be worked in curves and circles.

If the material used is of very loose weave, and frays easily, a tiny turning may be made on the right side and the punchstitching worked over that. Then the wrong side is trimmed close.

When attaching lace using this stitch, tack the lace onto the right

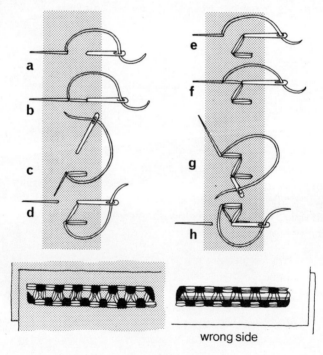

wrong side

60

side of the garment. Work the punchstitch over the foot edge of the lace into the garment. The surplus fabric underneath the lace may be trimmed back to the punchstitching afterwards.

The same method is employed when using the stitch for appliqué. The piece of material to be applied is tacked onto the background and the design lightly pencilled onto this applied piece. The punchstitching is then worked, and the surplus of the applied piece trimmed away to the stitching.

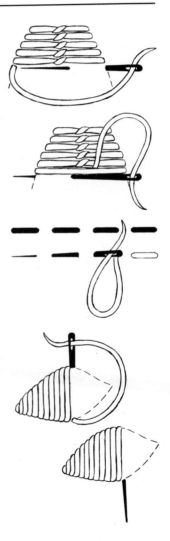

Roman stitch makes a filling or border stitch and can be graduated in size for suitable effects. It only differs from Roumanian stitch in the size of the centre stitch which is longer in Roumanian stitch.

Running stitch Basic stitch can be further elaborated, like back stitch, by **threading** or **whipping**.

Satin stitch perhaps second only to lazy daisy in popularity, makes a flat close cover with the stitches lying very close together. For the best result care needs to be taken that the thread does not become twisted. It is advisable to work it in a frame with two movements of the needle: first down through the fabric and second up through from the back. This makes the placing of the stitches much more accurate, particu-

larly on a closely woven fabric where the stitch is not being worked by the thread. It may be worked from right to left, or from left to right. Satin stitch may also be whipped, as in the diagram (left).

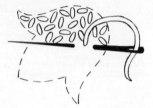

Seeding stitch is a useful filling stitch. It is made up of tiny straight stitches placed at different angles to each other but all of the same size. Care should be taken not to form a pattern but to keep the placing of stitches irregular.

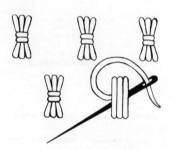

Sheaf filling stitch is made up from three vertical satin stitches bound round the middle by two overcast stitches which do not enter the material. It is used as a spot filling stitch.

Split stitch is a line stitch based on back stitch. The second stitch emerges from the middle of the first stitch thus splitting the thread of the first stitch. It makes a narrower line than stem stitch, and is more accurate in following sharply curved lines. It can be used as a shading stitch by working successive lines close up to each other in shades of one colour.

Stem stitch is perhaps the most widely used line stitch and it is basically a form of back stitch. Worked from left to right a small running stitch is taken along the line to be worked and the needle then comes up for the second stitch halfway back along its own length and to the left of the first stitch. The second stitch is of the same length as the first and takes the line half a stitch length beyond the first. The stitches may all be worked exactly on one line each stitch pushing the last slightly to the right. It can be used for shading by working successive rows close up to each other in different shades.

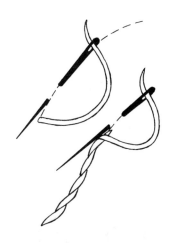

Straight stitch It seems perhaps too obvious a stitch to mention, but although easy it is a legitimate stitch in its own right. Care should be taken not to make the stitches too long or they will catch and be 'loopy'.

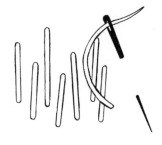

Thorn stitch is another useful stitch for a floral design. A long thread is taken through to the top of the material and left hanging loose like a couched thread to follow the chosen design line. It is taken to the back only at the end. The thorns are worked over this from side to side.

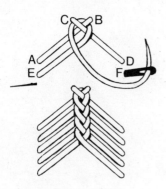

Vandyke stitch is a useful filling or border stitch. The size can be varied for leaf shapes. The needle comes out at **A** and enters the material at **B** and re-emerges at **C**. It then crosses to enter **D**, coming out again at **E**. Thereafter the needle passes under the loop of the centre and does not take up any material at the centre only re-entering the material at the far side at **F**. Continue.

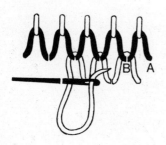

Wave stitch can be a useful filling stitch for shading. The first line is made up of straight stitches. The second line starts at **A** and threads under the first stitch of the first line, not taking up any material. A tiny stitch is then taken into the material at **B** and a second 'wave' is threaded under the second stitch of the first line, and so on. In the next row the 'wave' slips under *two* threads of the line before. It can be worked either close or open for a lacier effect.

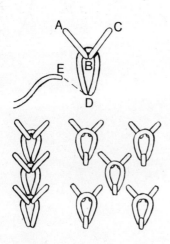

Wheatear stitch This stitch is worked towards the worker. Coming out at **A**, put the needle in at **B** and pass underneath emerging at **C** back to **B** and out at **D**. Then the thread is slipped under the two spiked ears and re-enters the material at **D**, then out at the top of the left hand spike **E**. This can be worked as a detached spot filling by working the two spiked 'ears' and then working a detached chain *over* the base of them.

A **spider's web** makes a very attractive spot filling, or a centre point. The spokes of the web are laid first. Then using a blunt needle fill in the web. Bring the thread up as near the centre as possible between **A** and **G**. Slip the needle under **A** and **E**, then back over **E** and under **D**, back over **D** and under **H**, and so on in ever widening circles until the web is complete. The web may be worked close, or open, for a more spidery effect.

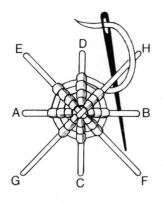

Trimmings and finishes

The finishing of any hand-made article is extremely important to its final appearance. A cushion without some kind of cord or fringe trimming can look quite naked and this will detract from the beauty and excellence of the embroidery, or if it is plain, of the fabric. The edging does not have to be particularly elaborate; a simple finish is often the most effective. Trimmings can of course be bought, but good quality ones are expensive and may be hard to match with the predominant colours of the embroidery. Hand-made trimmings can be made using the threads of the embroidery for a perfect finish. More elaborate edges can be made using lace, crochet and macramé techniques, which are not described here.

Cords

1 **A twisted cord.** This needs the help of a second person. Using two pencils, or two knitting needles, the one end of a thread of the desired colour round one needle, then make a long loop of the thread round both needles several times. The loop or ring must be about three times the required finished length of the cord, and the thread must be looped round as many times as will amount to about half the required finished thickness.

Then the two people twist their needles round and round in opposite directions, keeping the threads between them pulled tight meanwhile. Continue with this twisting until it is impossible to prevent the cord from forming little kinks despite the pull on it. Then hang a weight over the centre of the cord and bring the two needles together. The two halves will then spiral together. Knot another

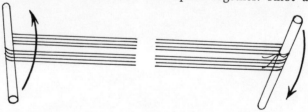

thread very tightly around the join and remove the needles and the weight. Do not stint on the twisting or the spiral will be loose and not evenly tight along its whole length.

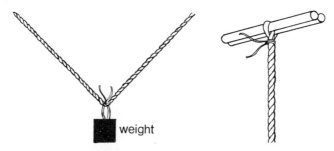

weight

This cord looks very attractive if made in two close shades of one colour, and it is an effective trimming for boxes and cushions. It can be made with any strong thread.

2   Another type of cord is a **finger cord** made of two strands of thread looped and knotted with the fingers. Tie the two ends of thread together and, making a loop with the left-hand thread, pull a loop of the right-hand thread through it—this loop coming through to the front from behind. Repeat, bringing a loop of the first thread through the second loop, and so on alternately. As these loops have to be large enough to pull the next one through with the finger, the tension will need adjusting between each looping. When each loop has been pulled through, the one before must be carefully pulled tight to form a firm cable cord. With practice some speed may be worked up. This cord is very effective in two colours, and is strong and firm enough for a drawstring tie, but is less well 'blended together' as an edging cord.

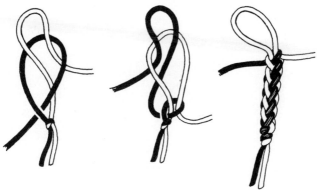

Fringes

1 In some cases the finish needs to be on the edge in the form of a fringe. A self-fringe is the easiest of all to make and is an effective finish to mats or cloths of any kind where a hem is not required. Draw a thread the desired length of the fringe from the edge of the fabric,

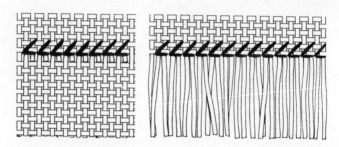

and hemstitch on the inside edge of this drawn ladder. Then pull and fray away all the crossing horizontal threads up to the line of the hemstitching.

2 If a hem or a seam has been made in the article, a fringe may still seem to be necessary for a perfect finish. Thread a loop of thread into the needle and taking a small stitch into the edge of the fabric pass the cut ends through the loop and cut off the desired length of the fringe **a**. Repeat.

3 This simple fringe can be made more elaborate by knotting the bundles together in twos along the first row, and then in a second row divide the knotted bundles of the first row and knot them again making alternate bundles **b**. A simple overhand knot may be used.

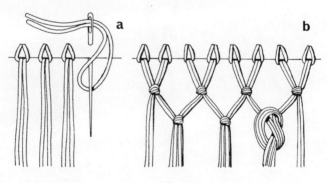

Tassels

Tassels will often be necessary on the ends of drawstring ties or cords, or on the corners of cushions. Again there are obviously degrees of elaboration possible, but the basic method is quite simple.

First find, or make a gauge the required length of the tassel. This may be a ruler, or a specially prepared piece of strong card. Wind a length of silk, or the chosen thread, round this gauge until enough thickness has been wound on to give the tassel the right amount of body. Then pass a threaded needle through under the silk next to the card at one edge. Tie the two ends together tightly. Cut the tassel off the card at the opposite side of the gauge. Thread the cut ends of a loop of the matching thread through a needle and, passing it round the tassel a little way down from the tied end, pass the needle through the loop and pull tight, forming a 'head' to the tassel. It is usually as well to secure this neck to the head a second time very firmly, and the end may then go up through the head and be used to attach the tassel. The first thread knotted through the tassel to hold it may now be cut off. The thread used to tie the neck of the tassel, while probably matching in colour may be of a firmer less silky twist than that used for the tassel itself.

This basic tassel may be elaborated by padding the head with a little ball of stuffing. The head may then be embroidered with rows of

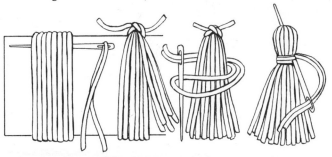

interlaced blanket stitch, perhaps in a contrasting colour. First work one row of blanket stitch at the very top of the dome of the head in a circle, all the upright stitches being taken into the centre. The stitches should not be pulled at all tight. The last stitch of the row joins into the first. Then bring the needle out a fraction below the first row and work a second row of blanket stitch with the vertical stitches going over the horizontal stitches of the row above. As the head of the tassel widens it is probable that two stitches will have to be worked into each one of the row above.

Repeat down to the neck. If the head was padded, the last rows may have to show a decrease in the number of blanket stitches as the head gets narrower as it nears the neck. This blanket network may be worked very closely or with the stitches lying further apart allowing the basic tassel head to show through.

If the tassel is to be attached to a cord, the end of the cord should be taken into the head of the tassel before the neck is tied. Then the thread used to tie the neck can be sewn firmly into the end of the cord. Or the end of the thread used for the cord may then be used to tie around the neck, thus making sure that tassel and cord become as nearly indissolubly joined as possible.

Pompoms

These are sometimes preferred as an alternative to tassels on draw string ties. There are several methods of making these but I prefer the following as it seems to me to ensure a more satisfactory result.

First prepare two identical circles of card of the size required for the pompom. These circles of card must have a central hole large enough for the amount of thread to pass through the number of times necessary to cover the rest of the card, thickly. The central hole most not be too big, as the ball will have a pile only the depth of the remaining outer band of card. Place the circles together; thread the needle with a double thread of the required colour and wind it through

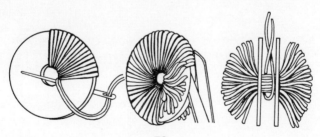

70

the hole and over the card round the ring until it is thickly covered. The end is secured by winding over it. Experience will show how thick the layer of winding must be; this will vary according to taste and to the thickness of thread used. The central hole may be nearly filled. The winding must be regularly and evenly done if the final result is to be satisfactory.

When the whole circle is covered, insert scissors in between the two pieces of cardboard and cut the threads where they pass over the edge. Then gently easing the two circles apart just a little more, pass a thread round the strands of thread between them and tie tightly. Repeat this for firmness. Then carefully strip away the cardboard circles and fluff up the pompom.

Other edgings

Some of the specialized embroidery techniques result in an article or garment which requires a little extra finish but may not need one of the edgings previously described. For instance, a smocked child's garment very often needs a little extra touch of embroidery on the collar to balance the fairly rich effect of the smocking of the yoke. One or two suitable edgings are given below.

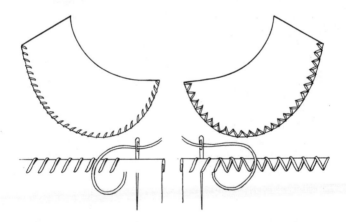

A simple whipped or overcast edging in the predominant colour is effective; or the overcasting may be worked in both directions to a depth of 3–5 mm (⅛″). First work in one direction all round, then return, completing the 'V's. Take the needle over the edge of the collar and enter the under side 3–5 mm (⅛″) along, and the same distance in. Return at a sloping angle a further 3–5 mm (⅛″) along and in, and bring the needle through to the upper side. This edging may be completed by a row of french knots.

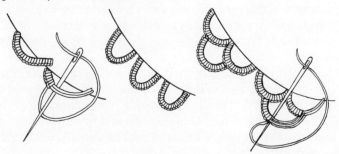

Another very delightful edging to a collar is a little buttonhole shell-shaped picot. Bring the needle out between the layers of the collar fabric and make two or three small loops along the edge of the collar 0·5 cm ($\frac{1}{4}''$) and entering 2 mm ($\frac{1}{16}''$) in from the edge, returning between the layers of the collar. Then buttonhole along this loop. These picots can of course be made in any shape which attracts the fancy—round or even double depending on the needs of the garment and the taste of the worker.

Another instance where a different kind of embroidered finish may set off an article is on a cushion embroidered in counted embroidery stitches. An alternative to an added fringe or cord is to work a row of one of the stitches through both the back and the front of the cushion forming a hem as on a pillowcase. This must be allowed for when making up the cushion as it will make it that much smaller.

Having completed the face of the cushion, sew it to the back, right sides together, taking care that the seam is straight along the thread of the fabric. Leave half of one side for the opening. Turn to the right side and tack a line of stitches parallel to the opening and the desired depth of the hem. Work the chosen embroidery stitch over this line on the front only so that it does not have to be unpicked when removing the pad to wash the cover. The end of the thread may be left ready to continue this stitch round the rest of the cushion.

Next tack the back and front together the same depth in from the seam line as already worked at the opening. The tacking acts as a guide line for the embroidery. If it is well covered it may be left in, so work it small and very neatly, again taking great care that it lies along the thread on both back and front if possible, and joins the stitching already worked over the opening. Then work the chosen stitch round the cushion cover through both layers. This may be a simple satin stitch border worked over different numbers of threads. Insert the pad and neatly and invisibly slip stitch the opening. Then back stitch the back of the cushion onto the front behind the single layer of embroidery so that it may be easily unpicked but does not show.

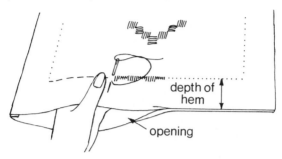

Hems

A hem has one main purpose. This is to neaten the edge of the material by folding in the rough edge with a double fold and sewing it down neatly, at the same time adding weight or body to the edge of the garment or article.

1 **Hemstitching** In some cases the hem is an integral part of the decoration of the article. This is particularly true of table and bed linen, and handkerchiefs, where the hem lies straight along the thread of the material. For this purpose hemstitching is most suitable.

The width of the fold or hem will vary according to the purpose and size of the article and the thickness of the fabric. A lady's handkerchief of lawn will look best if the hem is really narrow, 0·5 cm ($\frac{1}{4}$") or less; a linen tablecloth hem will be wider, say 2–3 cm (1"–1$\frac{1}{4}$"). It will also make a difference if the hem is the only decoration. If it is, the hem may be wider and more significant than if it is only a part of the decoration. No hard and fast rule can be laid down.

Hemstitching is usually worked in a thread of approximately the same thickness as the threads of the fabric being worked. A very narrow hem does not need to be tacked. It is easier for the embroideress to turn it by the thread as she goes along. A hem of 1 cm ($\frac{1}{2}$") or more may be tacked before it is worked. It is important for the finished result that the hem should be the same number of threads in width along the whole length. Therefore it must be so carefully folded and creased that **one** thread lies along the outside fold, and **one** thread, the required distance in, should lie along the edge of the inner fold exactly parallel to **one** thread of the underneath fabric.

This thread of the underneath fabric is carefully withdrawn bit by bit, to avoid pull, along the length of the hem **a**. With a very narrow hem this thread may be withdrawn bit by bit, a little ahead of the hemstitching. It will depend on the thickness of the fabric whether a second thread, or even a third, is withdrawn. A fairly simple rule is that single hemstitching may be worked when only one or two threads are withdrawn; double hemstitching (i.e. at both sides of the withdrawn ladder) should be worked when between three and five threads are withdrawn. If six or more threads are withdrawn some kind of more fancy drawn thread stitch should be worked on the withdrawn ladder. If there is a corner, as on table linen, this thread should be withdrawn to only about 2–3 cm ($1''$–$1\frac{1}{4}''$) from the inside corner and there left as a tail until the corner is prepared for mitring. (See page 77.)

For working hemstitching it is easiest to hold the work with the hem towards the worker, and to work from left to right. However it is more 'correct' to hold the work with the hem away from one, and to work from right to left. With some types of linen this gives a more satisfactory stitch. A compromise is to hold the work with the hem lying vertically away from the worker and to work towards her.

Secure the thread under the fold of the hem with a tiny back stitch and a few running stitches, and bring it out from the hem two threads from the edge of the inner fold. Counting carefully, insert the needle under the next two threads (or the required number according to the thickness) of the ladder left by the withdrawn threads **b**.

Pull the thread through gently holding it firmly away from one. Then crossing over these two threads insert the needle under the folded edge of the hem bringing it up two threads in beneath the bunch just formed **c**. Pull the thread tight. Repeat **d**.

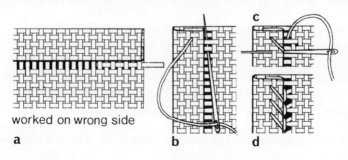

worked on wrong side

a   **b**   **c**   **d**

2 **A rolled hem** is used on very fine materials such as pure silk, organza or very fine lawn. A line of very small running stitches may be worked first about 2–3 mm ($\frac{1}{8}''$) from the edge, using a No 9 or 10 needle and pure silk thread. The edge is held away from the worker and the hem is worked from right to left. With the thumb and forefinger moistened, roll the edge a little at a time towards one into a very fine roll. This is then hemmed with the smallest possible stitches, taking up only one thread of the fabric **a**. Or the roll may be whipped. Insert the needle at a slant under the roll bringing it out at the back of the hem slightly to the left on the right side of the material **b**. Bring the

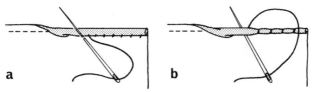

thread back over the tiny hem thereby keeping the roll in position. Again insert the needle under the roll and bring out through the back of the hem. Repeat. Pull the thread quite firm.

3 **A shell-edged hem** is used on lingerie or baby clothes in fine soft materials where an ordinary hemmed edge would look clumsy or be inclined to become frilly. The first fold should be as narrow as possible and the hem itself very narrow, 3–5 mm ($\frac{1}{8}''$). It is helpful to tack the hem down. The hem is held away from the worker and sewn from right to left. First take two or three tiny hemming stitches along the hem. Next, take the thread straight over the top of the hem and insert the needle into the right side of the material. Bring it out close to the edge of the hem on the wrong side. Pull this stitch tight. Make another overcast stitch and pull this tight also. Repeat at small regular intervals.

4 **A buttonholed hem** is in fact not a hem nor is it buttonholed. It is not a proper hem because the edge is not folded under. The stitching is

worked over the raw edge or, in some instances, is worked inside the edge and the edge trimmed close to the stitching afterwards. The stitch used is blanket stitch, which is buttonholing with each stitch separated by a gap of suitable proportion to the size of the stitch and the thickness of the fabric. This stitch is most commonly used on blankets or other thick materials which do not fray unduly, or as finish to a fine seam; or worked very closely as a decorative edge, sometimes scalloped. When worked on thick fabrics the stitches may be placed up to 0·5 cm (¼″) apart and are 1–1·5 cm (⅝″) deep.

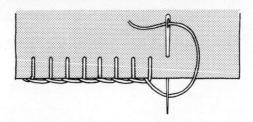

Holding the edge towards the worker, insert the needle 1 cm (½″) from the edge of the top side, bringing the needle out underneath the material at right angles to the edge and passing through the last loop formed. Repeat. When using blanket stitch to finish a fine seam such as a single pinstitched seam, the seam and therefore the blanket stitch will be on a much finer scale—say 2–3 mm (⅛″).

When the buttonholed edge is the finish for a child's dress, or piece of table linen, it must be worked very close together, with no space at

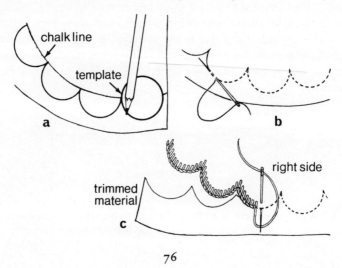

all between the stitches. This edge may also be scalloped as it gives a very pretty line; it is then worked as follows. The scalloped line should be drawn carefully first. If a template of a single scallop, or even circle, is first drawn the decoration can be fitted round a curve. First draw the line to be scalloped on the material in tailor's chalk. Then holding the template (a 10p piece may be a good size) on the line, draw halfway round it, and repeat **a**. This outline should then be worked in small running stitches **b**. Do not cut the material at this stage.

Next work the close buttonhole stitch over the line, making the needle come up very close on the outside of the line of running stitches, and with the stitches close together and of even tension. When the stitching is complete trim away the surplus material taking great care not to damage the stitching **c**.

Mitring

Square corners on household linen or handkerchiefs, or other hemmed corners, are usually mitred. This gives a good well-shaped corner without too much bulk under the hem, and is done exactly on the thread of the material.

The hem may first be worked up to 4–6 cm ($1\frac{1}{2}''$–$2''$) from the inside edge of the corner. Press a narrow fold on both sides of the corner along the same thread as the rest of the hem. Then turn the hem over to the required width on each side of the corner by the thread, and crease along the fold to the corner **a**.

Open out this hem crease and then turn down the corner diagonally on the crossing point of the hem creases.

Cut off surplus material from the corner **b**. Fold on hem creases

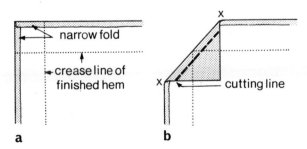

again thus bringing the two Xs to meet together. Tack corner ready for hemming or hemstitching **c**. Finish the mitred corner with an antique seam.

When hemstitching, the threads are normally withdrawn as far as the inside edge of the hem at the mitred corner, and not across the width of the hem as well. The ends are invisibly tucked under the hem. This leaves a little hole where the withdrawn threads coincide at the corner **d**.

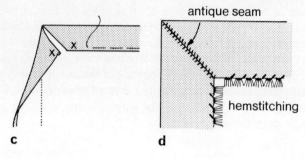

antique seam

hemstitching

c

d

78

Stockists

Mary Allen, Wirksworth, Derbyshire, DE4 4BN. Linens, canvas, metal threads, Appletons wool and D.M.C. threads.

Mace & Nairn, 89 Crane Street, Salisbury, Wilts, SP1 2PY. Linen, fabrics, canvas, metal threads, Anchor and D.M.C. threads, Appletons wools, Swedish linen threads, beeswax.

Royal School of Needlework, 25 Princes Gate, London, SW7 1QE. Metal threads and wools.

The Silver Thimble, 33 Gay Street, Bath, Avon, BA1 2NT.

Ells & Farrier, 5 Princes Street, Hanover Square, London, W1. Beads and jewels.

Christine Riley, 53 Barclay Street, Stonehaven, Kincardineshire, AB3 2AR. Threads, linens, metal threads, books.